IXTAPA & ZIHUATANEJO

BRUCE WHIPPERMAN

Contents

IXTAPA & ZIHUATANEJO

IXTAPA & ZIHUATANEJO

The resort pair of Ixtapa and Zihuatanejo present an irresistible opportunity for a season of relaxed vacationing. The choices seem nearly endless. You can sun to your heart's content on luscious beaches, choose from a feast of delicious food, and shop from a trove of fine Mexican handicrafts. Furthermore, outdoor lovers can enjoy their fill of unhurried beach walking and snorkeling, bicycling, horseback riding, kayaking, swimming, surfing, scuba diving, and caving.

Whether you stay in Ixtapa or Zihuatanejo depends on your inclinations. Zihuatanejo still resembles the small fishing village it once was, with many reminders of old Mexico, and has a mix of small to medium-size hotels. Ixtapa, on the other hand, is for modern travelers who prefer the fashionable glitter of a luxuriously comfortable facility-rich hotel on a crystal-line strand. (On the other hand, where you stay may not really matter, because Ixtapa and Zihuatanejo are only five miles/8 km apart.)

PLANNING YOUR TIME

There's hardly a better place for a balmy winter vacation than the Ixtapa and Zihuatanejo coast, whether it be for simply a four- or five-day-long weekend or a month of Sundays.

If your stay is limited to four or five days, you'll still have time for some sunning and snoozing on the beach or by the pool, sampling some of the excellent Zihuatanejo restaurants, visiting the **Museo Arqueología de la Costa Grande,** browsing Zihuatanejo's irresistible

© COMMONS.WIKIMEDIA.ORG

HIGHLIGHTS

◀ Museo Arqueología de la Costa Grande: Zihuatanejo's first stop for history aficionados illustrates the prehistory of the Costa Grande with a treasury of dioramas, paintings, and precious locally discovered and donated artifacts (page 12).

◀ Playa La Ropa: Enjoy this best of all possible resort beaches, tucked along a golden mile of Zihuatanejo Bay's sheltered eastern flank (page 14).

◀ Playa Las Gatas: Only boat accessible, Playa Las Gatas seems like a remote south-seas island, a place where sun, sea, and sand and the rustle of the palms invite relaxation. When you get hungry, a lineup of *palapa* restaurants provide fresh seafood; for exercise, beach stalls rent snorkel gear, which you can use to acquaint yourself with squadrons of tropical fish a few steps offshore (page 14).

◀ *Teleférico* and Playa del Palmar: Late afternoon, stroll along Ixtapa's creamy resort beach, Playa del Palmar, to the south end where the *teleférico* will whisk you uphill for a panoramic sunset and cocktails and dinner at the El Faro view restaurant (page 15).

◀ Isla Grande: Visitors to this petite, pristine island jewel can enjoy three different beaches, Playa Cuachalatate, Playa Varadero, and Playa Coral, tucked into the island's three sheltered corners. A fourth beach – Playa Carey, for romantics only – is a petite sandy nook accessible by boat only on the island's wild open-ocean shore (page 16).

◀ Barra de Potosí: This rustic palm-shadowed village, with a grand, mangrove-laced,

wildlife-rich lagoon on one side and a luscious beach on the other, seems perfect for a spell of relaxed living (page 54).

◀ Troncones: Once an isolated fishing village on a coral-decorated shoreline, Troncones has become a winter refuge for a loyal cadre of sun-starved Americans and Canadians (page 56).

LOOK FOR **◀** TO FIND RECOMMENDED SIGHTS, ACTIVITIES, DINING, AND LODGING.

trove of handicrafts, and spending an afternoon at either secluded **Playa Las Gatas** or **Isla Grande.**

With more time, you can concentrate more on your individual interests. Handicrafts, for example, are a major Zihuatanejo specialty. Start with an hour or two at the tourist market on the west side of town, with many stalls stuffed with

tempting treasures from all over Guerrero and Mexico. Then spend the rest of the day browsing the top-pick private handicrafts shops, such as Casa Marina, Artesanías Olinalá, Cerámicas Tonalá, and Galería Maya.

On the other hand, active vacationers will want to get into Ixtapa and Zihuatanejo's great outdoors. You might start off with a day

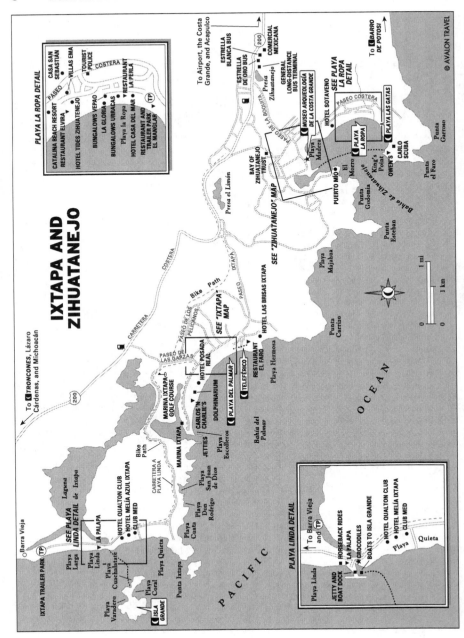

IXTAPA AND ZIHUATANEJO

sunning, hiking, and snorkeling off the beaches of Isla Grande. If you want more, you could try the same at Playa Las Gatas with a scuba-diving lesson thrown in. For still more outdoor adventures, do some bicycling on Ixtapa's new *ciclopista,* or head southeast to **Barra de Potosí** or northwest to **Troncones.**

With more days, head out of town south to Barra de Potosí for wildlife-viewing on the Laguna de Potosí or north to Troncones for sunning, swimming and surfing, and lingering a few nights at a comfortable bed-and-breakfast.

With a week or more, you'll have time to rent a car or take a taxi or bus northwest for an overnight or two in a comfortable **Troncones** beachfront bed-and-breakfast, or do the same by traveling southeast to **Barra de Potosí.** While in Troncones, adventurers will want to explore the limestone cave, do some deep-sea fishing, or maybe take a surfing lesson. At the village resort of Barra de Potosí, you can easily spend a couple of days sunning and beachcombing; dining on super-fresh seafood at rustic, palm-shaded *palapa* restaurants; and exploring, by boat or kayak, the grand, wildlife-rich Laguna de Potosí.

ORIENTATION
Both Ixtapa and Zihuatanejo are small and easy to know. Zihuatanejo's little Plaza de Armas town square overlooks the main beach, Playa Municipal, that fronts the palm-lined pedestrian walkway, Paseo del Pescador. From the plaza looking out toward the bay, you are facing south. On your right is the pier (*muelle,* moo-AY-yay), and on the left the bay curves along the outer beaches Playas La Ropa, Madera, and finally Las Gatas beneath the far Punta El Faro (Lighthouse Point).

Turning around and facing inland (north), you see a narrow but busy waterfront street, Juan Álvarez, running parallel to the beach past the plaza, crossing the main business streets (actually tranquil shady lanes) Cuauhtémoc and Guerrero. A third street, bustling Benito Juárez, one block to the right of Guerrero, conducts traffic several blocks to and from the shore, passing the market and intersecting a second main street, Avenida Morelos, about

10 blocks inland from the beach. There, a right turn will soon bring you to Highway 200 and, within five miles (8 km), Ixtapa.

Most everything in Ixtapa lies along one three-mile-long (5-km-long) boulevard, Paseo Ixtapa, which parallels the main beach, hotel-lined Playa del Palmar. Heading westerly, arriving from Zihuatanejo, you first pass the Club de Golf Ixtapa, then the big Hotel Barceló on the left, followed by a succession of other high-rise hotels. Soon come the Zona Comercial shopping malls and the Paseo de las Garzas corner on the right. Turn right for both Highway 200 and the outer Playas Cuata, Quieta, Linda, and Larga. At Playa Linda, boats continue to heavenly Isla Grande.

If, instead, you continued straight ahead from the Paseo de las Garzas corner, you would soon reach the Marina Ixtapa condo development and yacht harbor.

GETTING AROUND
In downtown Zihuatanejo, shops and restaurants are within a few blocks of the plaza. For the beaches, walk along the beachfront *andador* (walkway) to Playa Madera, take a taxi ($3) to Playa La Ropa, or take a launch from the pier ($5) to Playa Las Gatas.

For Ixtapa or the outer beaches, take a taxi (about $5) or ride one of the very frequent minibuses, labeled by destination, which leave from both Juárez, across from the market, and the northeast downtown corner of Juárez and Morelos, a few blocks farther north from the beach. In Ixtapa, walk or ride the minibuses that run along Paseo Ixtapa.

HISTORY
In the Beginning
The Purépecha-speaking people who lived in the area around A.D. 1400 were relative latecomers, preceded by waves of immigrants to Zihuatanejo. The local archaeological museum displays ancient pottery made by Zihuatanejo artisans as many as 5,000 years ago. Later, more sophisticated artists, influenced by the renowned Olmec mother-culture of the Gulf of Mexico coast, left their indisputable mark on local pottery styles.

PIRATES OF ZIHUATANEJO

For 10 generations, from the late 1500s to independence in 1821, corsairs menaced the Mexican Pacific coast. They often used Zihuatanejo Bay for repair and resupply.

The earliest was the renowned and feared English privateer Sir Francis Drake. During his circumnavigation of 1577-1580, Drake raided a number of Spanish Pacific ports.

The biggest prize, however, was the Manila galleon, for which he searched the Mexican coast for months. Finally, low on water and food, he dropped anchor and resupplied briefly at Zihuatanejo Bay before continuing northwest.

ENTER THE DUTCH

Dutch corsairs also scoured the seas for the Manila galleon. In October 1624, a Dutch squadron commanded by Captain Hugo Schapenham grouped in a semicircle outside Acapulco Bay to intercept the departing galleon. Port authorities, however, delayed the sailing, and the Dutch began running out of food and water. They tried to trade captives for supplies, but the Spanish refused, offering only inedible gold for the captives. In desperation, Schapenham tried to attack the Acapulco fort directly, but his vessels were damaged and driven off by the fort's effective artillery fire.

The starving Dutch sailors retreated up the coast to Zihuatanejo Bay where, after a few weeks, rested and resupplied, they set sail for Asia on November 29, 1624.

Although most of them arrived in the Moluccas Islands in the East Indies, they disbanded. Most of them, including Schapenham, who was dead by the end of 1625, never returned to Europe.

DAMPIER AND ANSON

A much more persistent and fortunate galleon hunter was English captain William Dampier (1651-1715), who, besides accumulating a fortune in booty, was renowned as a navigator and mapmaker. Lying in wait for the Manila galleon, Dampier anchored in Zihuatanejo Bay in 1704. On December 7, Dampier came upon the Manila galleon *Nuestra Señora del Rosario*.

By the beginning of the Christian era, local people had developed more sophisticated lifestyles. Instead of wandering and hunting and gathering their food, they were living in permanent towns and villages, surrounded by fields where they grew most of what they needed. Besides their staple corn, beans, and squash, these farmers, called Cuitlatecs by the Aztecs, were also cultivating tobacco, cotton for clothes, and cacao for chocolate. Attracted by the Cuitlatecs' rich produce, the highland Aztecs, led by their emperor Tizoc, invaded the coast during the late 1400s and extracted a small mountain of tribute yearly from the Cuitlatecs.

Conquest and Colonization

Scarcely months after Hernán Cortés conquered the Aztecs, he sent an expedition to explore the "Southern Sea" and find the long-sought route to China. In November 1522 Captain Juan Álvarez Chico set sail with boats built on the Isthmus of Tehuántepec and reconnoitered the Zihuatanejo coast all the way northeast to at least the Río Balsas, planting crosses on beaches and claiming the land for Spain.

Cortés, encouraged by the samples of pearls and gold that Chico brought back, built more ships and outfitted more expeditions. At a personal cost of 60,000 gold pesos (probably equivalent to several million dollars today) Cortés had three ships built at Zacatula, at the mouth of the Río Balsas. He commissioned Captain Álvaro Saavedra Cerón to command the first expedition to find the route to Asia. Saavedra Cerón set off from Zihuatanejo Bay on October 31, 1527. He commanded a modest force of about 110 men, with 30 cannons, in three small caravels: the flagship *Florida,* the *Espíritu Santo,* and the *Santiago.* The *Florida,* Saavedra Cerón's sole vessel to survive the fierce Pacific typhoons, reached present-day Guam on December 29, 1527, and the Philippines on February 1, 1528.

However, a ferocious Spanish defense forced Dampier's squadron to retreat.

Six years later, commanding another squadron jointly with Captain Woodes Rogers, Dampier captured both the galleon *Encarnación* and the *Nuestra Señora de Begoña* between January 1 and January 5, 1710. Rogers and Dampier returned triumphantly to England in the *Encarnación*, which they had rechristened the *Batchelor.*

Luckiest of all Manila galleon treasure hunters was George Anson (1697–1762), who volunteered for the English navy at the age of 15 and rose rapidly, attaining the rank of captain at the age of 25.

In command of a small fleet of ships and hundreds of sailors, he arrived off Acapulco on March 1, 1742. After waiting three weeks for the galleon to sail, and running low on food and water, Anson sailed northwest, resupplied at Zihuatanejo, and then departed west across the Pacific. On July 1, 1743, off Guam, Anson's forces caught up with and captured the galleon *Nuestra Señora de Covdonga*, with 1.3 million pieces of eight, 35,000 ounces of silver, and a trove of jewels. (A "piece of eight" is an old label for a famous Spanish coin, coveted by pirates the world over.)

Although suffering from the loss of 90 percent of his men, Anson finally returned to England in command of his last remaining ship, carrying booty worth 800,000 pounds sterling, a fortune worth many tens of millions of dollars today.

William Dampier, 1651-1715   **George Anson, 1697-1762**

As he did not know any details of the Pacific Ocean and its winds and currents, it's not surprising that Saavedra Cerón failed to return to Mexico. He died at sea in October 1529 in search of a return route to Mexico.

No fewer than seven more attempts were needed (from Acapulco in 1532, 1539, and 1540; Tehuántepec in 1535; and Barra de Navidad, two in 1542 and one in 1564) until finally, in 1565, navigator-priest Andrés de Urdaneta coaxed Pacific winds and currents to give up their secret and returned triumphantly to Acapulco from Asia.

The Manila Galleon

Thereafter, the trading ship called the Manila galleon sailed yearly from Acapulco for Asia. For more than 250 years, it returned to Acapulco within a year, laden with a fortune in spices, silks, gold, and porcelain. Although Acapulco's prominence all but shut down all other Mexican Pacific ports, the Manila galleon would from time to time stop off at Zihuatanejo. The same was true for the occasional pirate ship (or fleet) that lurked along the coast, hungry to capture the galleon's riches.

The most famous corsair was Francis Drake, who landed in Zihuatanejo in 1579. Later came the Dutch fleet of Hugo Schapenham in 1624. English Captain William Dampier entered Zihuatanejo Bay in 1704, recording that the shoreline village had about 40 grass huts, inhabited by about 100 unfriendly people who vigorously discouraged his disembarkation. The luckiest of all the corsairs was Captain George Anson, who, in 1715, captured the Manila galleon and returned to England with booty then worth 800,000 pounds sterling—upwards of $50 million today.

On one occasion, no one knows when exactly, a galleon evidently lost some of its precious silk cargo, which washed ashore on one of Zihuatanejo's beaches, now known as Playa La Ropa (Clothes Beach).

Independence

In 1821, Mexico won its independence, stopping the Manila galleon forever. Deprived even of an occasional galleon or pirate ship, Zihuatanejo went to sleep and didn't wake up for more than half a century. The occasion was the arrival of ex-president Lerdo de Tejada, who, during the 1870s, embarked from Zihuatanejo for exile in the United States.

By the 20th century, some of the maritime prosperity of Acapulco, which benefited from the stream of California-bound steamers, spilled over to Zihuatanejo. During the 1920s, nearby resources were exploited, and what is now known as Playa Madera (Wood Beach) earned its label as a loading point for fine hardwood timber exports.

Modern Ixtapa and Zihuatanejo

Recognition of Zihuatanejo's growing importance came on November 30, 1953, when the Guerrero state legislature decreed the formation of the Zihuatanejo *municipio,* whose governmental center was established at the budding town on the bay of the same name.

In the 1960s, a new airport suitable for propeller passenger airplanes, and the paved highway, which arrived from Acapulco around the same time, jolted Zihuatanejo (pop. 1,500) from its final slumber. No longer isolated, Zihuatanejo's headland-rimmed aqua bay began to attract a small colony people seeking paradise on earth.

Tourism grew steadily. Small hotels and restaurants were built to accommodate visitors. Zihuatanejo had a population of perhaps 5,000 by the late 1970s when Fonatur, the government tourism-development agency, decided to develop Zihuatanejo Bay. Local folks, however, objecting that the proposed lineup of high-rise hotels would block the view of their beautiful bay, squelched the plan.

Fonatur regrouped and alternatively proposed Ixtapa (often translated as White Place, but it more likely means White Top, for the several guano-topped offshore islets) five miles (8 km) north of Zihuatanejo as a perfect site for a world-class resort. Investors agreed, and the infrastructure—drainage, roads, and utilities—was installed. The jet airport was built, hotels rose, and by 2000, the distinct but inseparable twin resorts of Ixtapa and Zihuatanejo (combined pop. 80,000) were attracting a steady stream of Mexican and foreign vacationers.

Sights

◖ MUSEO ARQUEOLOGÍA DE LA COSTA GRANDE

Zihuatanejo's smallish but fine archaeological museum (Plaza Olaf Palme, Paseo del Pescador, tel. 755/554-7552, 10 A.M.–6 P.M. Tues.–Sun., $3) at the east end of the main town beach authoritatively details the prehistory of the Costa Grande. Professionally prepared maps, paintings, dioramas, and artifacts—many donated by local resident and innkeeper Anita Rellstab—illustrate the development of local cultures, from early hunting and gathering to agriculture and, finally, urbanization by the time of the conquest.

BEACHES AROUND ZIHUATANEJO BAY

Ringed by forested hills, edged by steep cliffs, and laced by rocky shoals, Zihuatanejo Bay would be beautiful even without its beaches. Five of them line the bay.

Playas El Almacén, Municipal, and Madera

Zihuatanejo Bay's west side shelters narrow, tranquil Playa El Almacén (Warehouse Beach), mostly good for fishing from its nearby rocks. Moving east past the pier toward town brings you to the colorful, bustling Playa Municipal.

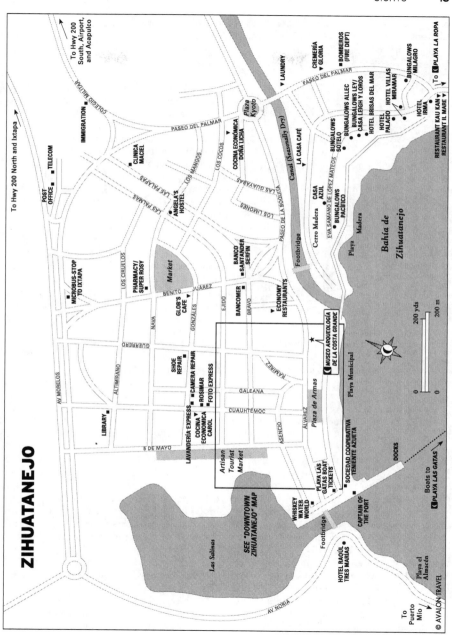

ZIHUATANEJO

To Hwy 200 North and Ixtapa

To Hwy 200 South, Airport, and Acapulco

COLEGIO MILITAR

POST OFFICE
TELECOM

IMMIGRATION

CLINICA MACIEL

LAS PALMAS
LAS PALMAS

ANGELA'S HOSTEL

PASEO DEL PALMAR

LOS COCOS
LOS MANGOS
LOS GUAYABAS
LOS LIMONES

COCINA ECONÓMICA DOÑA LUCHA

LA CASA CAFÉ

PASEO DE LA BOQUITA

Canal (Seasonally Dry)

LAUNDRY

Plaza Kyoto

CREMERÍA GLORIA
BOMBEROS (FIRE DEPT)
BUNGALOWS MILAGRO

PASEO DEL PALMAR

BUNGALOWS ALLEC
BUNGALOWS LEY/ CASA LEIGH Y LOROS
HOTEL VILLAS MIRAMAR
HOTEL BRISAS DEL MAR
HOTEL PALACIO
HOTEL IRMA

BUNGALOWS SOTELO

EVA SÁMANO DE LÓPEZ MATEOS

CASA AZUL
Cerro Madera
BUNGALOWS PACÍFICO

RESTAURANT KAU KAN
RESTAURANT IL MARE

To PLAYA LA ROPA

Playa Madera

Footbridge

Bahía de Zihuatanejo

MICROBUS-STOP TO IXTAPA

LOS CIRUELOS

PHARMACY/ SUPER ROSY

Market

BENITO JUÁREZ

GLOB'S CAFÉ

BANCO SANTANDER SERFIN

BANCOMER

NAVA
GONZALES
EJIDO
BRAVO

ECONOMY RESTAURANTS

200 yds
200 m
0
0

GUERRERO
ALTAMIRANO
AV MORELOS

SHOE REPAIR

CAMERA REPAIR
ROSIMAR
FOTO EXPRESS

LAVANDERÍA EXPRESS
COCINA ECONÓMICA CAROL

6 DE MAYO

RAMIREZ

GALEANA

CUAUHTÉMOC

ASENCIO
ÁLVAREZ

Plaza de Armas

MUSEO ARQUEOLOGÍA DE LA COSTA GRANDE

Playa Municipal

LIBRARY

Artisan Tourist Market

SEE "DOWNTOWN ZIHUATANEJO" MAP

WHISKEY WATER WORLD

PLAYA LAS GATAS BOAT TICKETS

SOCIEDAD COOPERATIVA TENIENTE AZUETA

DOCKS

Boats to PLAYA LAS GATAS

CAPTAIN OF THE PORT

Las Salinas

Footbridge

HOTEL RAOÚL TRES MARÍAS

AV NORIA

To Puerto Mío

Playa el Almacén

© AVALON TRAVEL

© BRUCE WHIPPERMAN

An easy beachfront walk leads from Playa Madera to Zihuatanejo's main town beach.

Its sheltered waters are fine for wading, swimming, and boat launching (which anglers, their motors buzzing, regularly do) near the pier end. For maximum sun and serenity, continue walking east away from the pier along Playa Municipal. Cross the pedestrian bridge over the usually dry Agua de Correa creek, which marks the east end of Playa Municipal. Continue along the concrete *andador* that winds about 200 yards along the beachfront rocks that run along the west end of Playa Madera. (If you prefer, you can also hire a taxi to take you to Playa Madera, about $3.)

Playa Madera (Wood Beach), once a loading point for lumber, stretches about 300 yards, decorated with rocky nooks and outcroppings and backed by the lush hotel-dotted hill **Cerro Madera.** The beach sand is fine and gray-white. Swells enter the facing bay entrance, usually breaking suddenly in two- or three-foot waves that roll in gently and recede with little undertow. Madera's usually calm billows are good for child's play and easy swimming. Bring your mask and snorkel for glimpses of fish in the clear waters. Beachside restaurant/bars at the Hotel Brisas del Mar and the Hotel Irma, above the far east end, serve drinks and snacks.

Playa La Ropa

Zihuatanejo Bay's favorite resort beach is Playa La Ropa (Clothes Beach), a mile-long crescent of yellow-white sand washed by oft-gentle surf. The beach got its name centuries ago from the apparel that once floated in from a galleon wrecked offshore. From the summit of the beach's clifftop approach road, **Paseo Costera,** the beach sand, relentlessly scooped and redeposited by the waves, appears as an endless line of half moons.

On the 100-foot-wide Playa la Ropa, vacationers bask in the sun, personal watercraft buzz beyond the breakers, rental sailboats ply the waves, and sailboards rest on the sand. The waves, generally too gentle and quick-breaking for surf sports, break close-in and recede with only mild undertow. With its broad horizon and *palapa* restaurants, it's a favorite spot to watch the sun go down. Joggers come out mornings and evenings.

Playa Las Gatas

Secluded Playa Las Gatas, reachable from Playa La Ropa by taxi and a rocky one-mile shoreline hike or much more easily by launch from the town pier, lies sheltered beneath the south-end Punta El Faro headland. Legend has it that the apparent line of rock rubble visible 200 feet off the beach is what remains of a walled-in royal bathing pool that the emperor of the Purépecha people (who still inhabit the highlands of Michoacán) had built to protect his family and friends from the small cat-whiskered nurse sharks that frequent the shoreline. Although the emperor is long gone, the sharks continue to swim off Playa Las Gatas (Cats Beach), named for the sharks' whiskers. (The nurse sharks, however, are harmless; moreover, Las Gatas scuba instructors Thierry and Jean-Claude Duran told me that authoritative archaeological investigators have shown that the rocks are a natural formation.)

Playa La Ropa's sun, sand, and gentle surf seem made for child's play.

Generally calm and quiet, often with super-clear offshore waters, Playa Las Gatas is both a surfing and snorkeling haven and a jumping-off spot for dive trips to prime scuba sites. Beach booths rent gear for beach snorkelers, and a professional dive shop right on the beach, Carlo Scuba, instructs and guides both beginner and experienced scuba divers. (For more diving details, see *Sports and Recreation*.)

For a treat (high season only, however), pass the beach restaurant lineup and continue to **Owen's** (cell tel. 044-755/102-7111, 8 A.M.–7 P.M. daily, closed Sept. and Oct.) *palapa* restaurant, visible on King's Point, the palm-shaded outcropping past the far curve of the beach. There, enjoy some refreshment, watch the surfers glide around the point, and feast on the luscious beach, bay, and hill views.

IXTAPA INNER BEACHES

Ixtapa's 10 distinct beaches lie scattered like pearls along a dozen miles of creamy, azure coastline. As you move from the Zihuatanejo end, **Playa Hermosa** comes first. The elevators

of the super-luxurious clifftop Hotel Brisas Ixtapa make access to the beach very convenient. At the bottom you'll find a few hundred yards of seasonally broad white sand, with open-ocean (but often gentle) waves usually good for most water sports except surfing. Good beach-accessible snorkeling is possible off the shoals at either end of the beach. Extensive rentals are available at the beachfront aquatics shop. A poolside restaurant serves food and drinks. Hotel access is only by car or taxi.

◖ *Teleférico* and Playa del Palmar

For a sweeping vista of Ixtapa's beaches, bay, and blue waters, ride the *teleférico* (cableway, 7 A.M.–11 P.M. daily) to **El Faro** (tel. 755/555-2510, 8 A.M.–10 P.M. daily in high winter–spring season, shorter hours low season, breakfast $5–10, lunch $8–15, dinner entrées $14–25), a view restaurant at the south end of Ixtapa's main beach, Playa del Palmar.

Long, broad, and yellow-white, Playa del Palmar could be called the Billion-Dollar Beach for the investment money it attracted to Ixtapa. The confidence seems justified. The broad strand stretches for three gently curving miles. Even though it fronts the open ocean, protective offshore rocks, islands, and shoals keep the surf gentle most of the time. Here, most sports are of the high-powered variety—parasailing ($25), personal watercraft riding and water-skiing ($50), and banana-tubing ($10)—although boogie boards can be rented for $5 an hour on the beach.

Challenging surfing breaks roll in consistently off the jetty at **Playa Escolleros**, at Playa del Palmar's far west end. Bring your own board.

IXTAPA OUTER BEACHES

Ixtapa's outer beaches spread among the coves and inlets a few miles northwest of the Hotel Zone. Drive, bicycle (rentals near the Hotel Emporio), taxi, or take a minibus marked Playa Linda along the Paseo de las Garzas. Drivers, heading east along the Ixtapa hotel row, at the end of the shopping complex, turn right, then fork left after a few hundred yards. After passing the Marina Golf Course (watch out for crocodiles crossing the road, no joke), the road turns toward the shoreline, winding past a trio of beach gems: Playa San Juan de Dios, Playa Don Rodrigo, and Playa Cuata. Sadly, development has now blocked access to these beaches.

Although Mexican law theoretically allows free public oceanfront access, guards might try to shoo you away from any one of these beaches on the open-ocean side, even if you arrive by boat. If somehow you manage to get there, you will discover cream-yellow strips of sand, nestled between rocky outcroppings, with oft-gentle waves and correspondingly moderate undertow for good swimming, bodysurfing, and boogie boarding. Snorkeling and fishing are equally good around nearby rocks and shoals.

On the peninsula's sheltered northern flank, **Playa Quieta** (Quiet Beach) is a place that lives up to its name: a tranquil, sheltered strand of clear water nestled beneath a forested hillside. A ribbon of fine yellow sand arcs around a smooth inlet dotted by a regatta of Club Med kayaks and sailboats plying the water. Get there via the north-end access stairway from the parking lot, signed Playa Quieta Acceso Público. Stop by the beachfront restaurant for refreshment or a fresh seafood lunch.

PLAYA LINDA

Playa Linda, the open-ocean yellow-sand beach at road's end, stretches for miles northwest, where it's known as Playa Larga (Long Beach). Flocks of sandpipers and plovers skitter at the surf's edge and pelicans and cormorants dive offshore while gulls, terns, and boobies skim the wavetops. Driftwood and shells decorate the sand beside a green-tufted palm grove that seems to stretch endlessly to the north.

In addition to the beach, mangrove-fringed **Laguna de Ixtapa,** an arm of which extends south to the bridge before the Playa Linda parking lot, is becoming an attraction. The lagoon's star actors are crocodiles that often sun and doze in the water and along the bank beneath the bridge.

Officially, the bicycle path ends at the bridge, but you can continue on foot or by bicycle about 1.5 miles (2.5 km) to Barrio Viejo village. Take a hat, water, insect repellent, your binoculars, and your bird-identification book. (For more bicycling information, see the *Sports and Recreation* section.)

The friendly downscale **La Palapa** beach restaurant, at pavement's end, offers beer, sodas, and seafood, plus showers, toilets, and free parking. Neighboring stable **Rancho Playa Linda** (11 A.M.–6 P.M. daily), managed by friendly "Spiderman" Margarito, provides horseback rides for about $20 per hour.

The flat, wide Playa Linda has powerful rollers often good for surfing. Boogie boarding and bodysurfing—with caution, don't try it alone—are also possible. Surf fishing yields catches, especially of *lisa* (mullet), which locals have much more success netting than hooking.

◖ ISLA GRANDE

Every few minutes a boat heads from the Playa Linda embarcadero to mile-long Isla Grande

Playa Linda (Beautiful Beach) always seems to live up to its name.

© BRUCE WHIPPERMAN

(formerly Isla Ixtapa, 9 A.M.–5 P.M. daily, $4 round-trip). Upon arrival, you soon discover the secret to the preservation of the island's pristine beaches, forests, and natural underwater gardens: "No trash here," the *palapa* proprietors say. "We bag it up and send it back to the mainland." And the effort shows. Great fleshy green orchids and bromeliads hang from forest branches, multicolored fish dart among offshore rocks, shady native acacias hang lazily over the shell-decorated sands of the island's little beaches.

Boats from Playa Linda arrive at **Playa Cuachalatate** (koo-ah-chah-lah-TAH-tay), the island's most popular beach, named for a local tree whose bark is said to relieve liver ailments. On the island's sheltered inner shore, it's a playground of crystal sand, clear water, and gentle ripples, perfect for families. Many visitors stay all day, splashing, swimming, and eating fresh fish, shrimp, and clams cooked at any one of a dozen beachfront *palapas*. Visitors also enjoy the many sports and equipment on offer: jet skis ($50/hr), banana-tube rides ($5),

fishing-boat rentals ($60/half day), aquatic bicycles ($6/hr), snorkel gear ($3/hr), and kayaks ($5/hr).

For a change of scene, follow the short concrete walkway over the west-side (to the right as you arrive) forested knoll to **Playa Varadero** and **Playa Coral** on opposite flanks of an intimate little isthmus. Varadero's yellow-white sand is narrow and tree-shaded, and its waters are calm and clear. Behind it lies Playa Coral, a steep coral-sand beach fronting a rocky blue bay. Playa Coral is a magnet for beach lovers, snorkelers, and the scuba divers who often arrive by boat to explore the waters around the offshore coral reef. Women offer massage to the soothing music of the waves ($25).

Isla Grande's fourth and smallest beach, secluded **Playa Carey,** is named for the sea-turtle species. An open-ocean dab of sand nestling between petite, rocky headlands, it's easily accessible by boat from Playa Cuachalatate, but not frequently visited.

Accommodations

The Ixtapa and Zihuatanejo area is one of the Mexican Pacific Coast's loveliest but also most highly seasonal resorts. Hotels and restaurants are most likely to be full during the sunny winter–spring high season, customarily beginning about December 20 and running through Easter week. Low season begins during the oft-hot dry months of May and June and continues until early December. Some restaurants even shut down during September and October. Nevertheless, for those who crave peace and quiet, bargain hotel prices, just-right balmy weather, and lush verdure, late fall—mid-October through mid-December—is an excellent time to visit. Hotel rates listed here as "low season" are the prices for two that you'll often encounter May through November. Prices listed as "high season" or "holidays" are the steeper tariffs that you will generally encounter during the Christmas–New Year's holidays, often extending through the Easter holiday. Hotels listed here are grouped by location—for Zihuatanejo, Downtown Zihuatanejo, Playa La Madera, and Playa La Ropa, and for Ixtapa, Ixtapa and Playa Linda—and generally listed in ascending order of low-season price.

Zihuatanejo and Ixtapa hotels divide themselves by location (and largely by price) between the budget-to-moderate downtown and more expensive Playa Madera, Playa La Ropa, and Ixtapa. For more information on Zihuatanejo and Ixtapa lodgings, visit the excellent websites www.zihuatanejo.net and www.ixtapa-zihuatanejo.net, or the individual hotel websites listed. Although Zihuatanejo hotels (with the few exceptions noted) provide little or no wheelchair access, all accommodations described in the *Ixtapa* section do.

IXTAPA OR ZIHUATANEJO?

Your choice of local lodging sharply determines the tone of your stay. Zihuatanejo still resembles the colorful seaside village that visitors have enjoyed for years. Fishing *pangas* decorate its beach side, while *panaderías, taquerías,* and *papelerías* line its narrow shady lanes. Many of its hotels – budget to moderate, with spartan but clean fan-only rooms – reflect the tastes of the bargain-conscious travelers who "discovered" Zihuatanejo during the 1960s.

Ixtapa, on the other hand, mirrors the fashionwise preferences of new-generation Mexican and international vacationers. A broad boulevard fronts your Ixtapa hotel, while on the beach side thatch-shaded chairs on a wide strand, a palmy garden, blue pool, and serene outdoor restaurant are yours to enjoy. Upstairs, your air-conditioned room – typically in plush pastels, with private sea-view balcony, marble bath, room service, and your favorite TV shows by satellite – brings maximum convenience and comfort to a lush tropical setting.

Actually, you needn't be forced to choose. Split your hotel time between Ixtapa and Zihuatanejo and enjoy both worlds.

DOWNTOWN ZIHUATANEJO
Under $50

Right in the middle of the downtown beachfront action is **Casa de Huéspedes Elvira** (Paseo del Pescador 9, tel. 755/554-2061, casa-elvira@hotmail.com, $15 s or d, $25 holidays), operated since 1956 by its founder, Elvira R. Campos. Every day, Elvira looks after her little garden of flowering plants, feeds rice to her birds—both wild and caged—and passes the time with friends and guests. She tells of the "way it used to be" when all passengers and supplies arrived from Acapulco by boat, local *almejas* (clams) were as big as cabbages, and you could pluck fish right out of the bay with your hands. Her petite eight-room lodging divides into an upstairs section, with more light and privacy, and a lower, with private baths. The leafy, intimate lower patio leads to the airy upper level via a pair of quaint plant-decorated

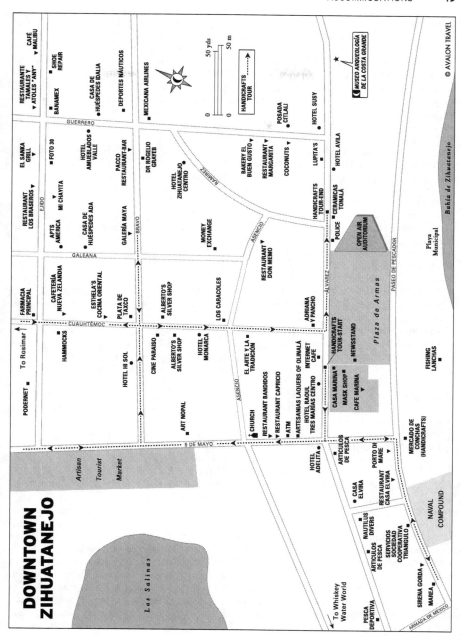

DOWNTOWN ZIHUATANEJO

© AVALON TRAVEL

spiral staircases. The rooms themselves are small, authentically rustic, and clean. The four upper rooms share a bathroom and toilet. Rates run about $15 s or d, $25 t low season and $25 and $30 holidays. If nighttime noise bothers you, bring earplugs; TV and music from Elvira's adjoining restaurant continues until about 11 P.M. most evenings during the winter high season.

On the west side, across the lagoon mouth by footbridge from the end of Paseo del Pescador, is the **Hotel Raoúl Tres Marias** (Noria 4, Colonia Lázaro Cárdenas, tel. 755/554-2591 or 755/554-2191, $25 d). Its longtime popularity derives from its budget prices and the colorful lagoon-front boat scene, visible from porches outside some of its 25 rooms. Otherwise, facilities are strictly bare-bones, with only room-temperature water. Rooms rent for $20 s, $30 d, $35 t low season and $40 s, $50 d, $60 t holidays, with fans and most with private baths.

A few blocks north and west, find unpretentious guesthouse **(Casa de Huéspedes Idalia** (Guerrero 9, tel. 755/554-2062, $20 d). The grandmotherly owner offers two floors of about a dozen plain but clean rooms, with room-temperature-only shower baths. Idalia's guests enjoy an airy upstairs corridor-view porch, furnished with hammocks, rocking chairs, and shelves of thick paperback books. Rentals go for $15 s, $20 d, with fans only, or $30 s or d, with air-conditioning and TV, $40 for refrigerator.

Behind the town market, tucked on a quiet side street about five blocks from the beach, budget-conscious travelers will appreciate the attractive **(Angela's Hotel and Hostel** (Ascencio 10, local cell tel. 044-755/112-2191, angelashostel@hotmail.com, www.zihuatanejo .com.mx/angelas, $25 d, $35 t, $12 dorm), competently managed by friendly Angela Villalobos and Gregg Thompson. They offer a range of clean, invitingly rustic fan-only accommodations, including private rooms with beds for kids and dormitories (male, female, and mixed). Extras include a shady plant-decorated hammock-hung veranda, fine for relaxing and socializing.

Back downtown, a block from the beach, **Hotel Susy** (corner of Guerrero and Álvarez, tel./fax 755/554-2339, viajesbravo@yahoo.com) offers three floors of rooms around a shady inner patio. The seven upper-floor bayside rooms have private view balconies. Inside corridors unfortunately run past room windows, necessitating closing curtains for privacy, a drawback in these fan-only rooms. Avoid traffic noise by requesting an upper-floor room away from the street. The 20 clean but plain rooms go for $30 s, $40 d (in one bed), $50 d or t (in two beds) low season, and $40, $52, and $65 holidays, including fans and private hot-water baths.

Next door, another good moderately priced choice, if you don't mind a bit of morning noise from the adjacent school, is the popular **(Posada Citlali** (Guerrero 3, tel./fax 755/554-2043, $40 d). The hotel (Citlali means star in Náhuatl) rises in a pair of three-story tiers around a shady plant-decorated inner courtyard. The 20 plain, rather small, but clean rooms are all thankfully removed from direct street-traffic hubbub. Guests on the upper floors experience less corridor traffic and consequently enjoy more privacy. Reservations are mandatory during the high season and strongly recommended at other times. Rates run about $35 s, $40 d, $45 t low season and $40 s, $50 d, $55 t holidays, with private hot-water baths and fans.

A block west, on a leafy car-free lane, stands Ada Aburto Pineda's modest guesthouse, **(Casa de Huéspedes Ada** (Galeana 14, tel. 755/554-2186, nos@prodigy.net.mx, $25–80). Her seven rentals differ markedly. Downstairs, she offers three plain, dark, and small (barely recommendable) but clean rooms, two with fans, one with air-conditioning, for about $25 d. Her four upstairs accommodations are much larger, lighter, and more recommendable. Two are airy, multiroom kitchenette apartments with fans, accommodating up to four or five people. They open to a spacious, leafy front porch overlooking the shady street scene below. The two remaining upstairs units are in the rear and are smaller but still comfortable and clean, with fans and double beds. The larger of the two has a kitchenette. The big upstairs apartments rent for $60 d low season, $80 d high, or $700/month in low season, $1,400 high. The smaller upstairs kitchenette goes for $40 d low, $70 d high, or $400/month low, $900 high; the nonkitchenette, $35 d low, $45 d high. All units come with private baths, TV, and parking.

$50-100

At the center of Zihuatanejo street hubbub is **Hotel Monarca** (Cuauhtémoc 13, tel./fax 755/554-2030 or 744/553-2922, $50 d). Choose from six attractive kitchenette (microwave only) studios in three floors. Units are clean, airy, and comfortable; two have private view balconies. They accommodate two to four people with combinations of double and single beds. Rentals run a reasonable $45 d low season, $65 holidays, $1,200 per month, all with TV, refrigerator, fans, and coffeemaker.

About three blocks from the beach, find **Hotel Amueblados Valle** (Guerrero 33, tel. 755/554-2084, fax 755/554-3220). Inside the front door, find eight furnished apartments, in three floors around an invitingly green inner patio. The apartments themselves, all with kitchens and either one or two bedrooms and shower baths, are clean, spacious, and comfortably appointed. Upper apartments are breezier and lighter. One-bedroom units go for about $50 low, $85 high season; two bedrooms, about $60 low, $95 high season. Discounts are possible for monthly rentals. All with TV and fans, but no parking.

Its location near the town pier draws many fishing enthusiasts to the **Hotel Raoúl Tres Marías Centro** (Juan Álvarez and Cinco de Mayo, tel./fax 755/554-6706, reservatresmarias@prodigy.net.mx, www.ixtapa-zihuatanejo.net/r3marias/, $68 s or d). Some of the 18 rooms have private balconies looking out on the street below. Newcomers might pick up some local fishing pointers after dinner at the hotel's restaurant, Los Garrobos. Rooms are $115 at holidays, and all come with hot water, cable TV, air-conditioning, and credit cards accepted.

Right in the middle of everything is Mexican family favorite **Hotel Zihuatanejo Centro** (Ramírez 2, tel. 755/554-2669, fax 755/554-6897, zihuacenter@prodigy.net.mx, www.ixtapa-zihuatanejo.net/zihuacenter, credit cards accepted, $70 s or d, $90 holidays), Although it's right smack downtown, about two blocks from the beach, guests are nevertheless sheltered from the street noise by rooms that face inward onto an inviting inner pool-courtyard. The 79 rooms, rising in four stories, are clean and simply but comfortably furnished in pastels and vinyl floor tile. Some rooms have two double beds, others have one king- or queen-sized bed. For more air and light, ask for a room with a balcony. Rates run about $85 s or d, with balcony, $70 without; $120 and $90 holidays (ask for a promotional package); with air-conditioning, fans, cable TV, hot-water shower baths, parking, restaurant, and credit cards accepted.

A block west, guests at **Apartments America** (Galeana 16, tel. 755/554-4337, zihuatanejoamerica7@hotmail.com, www.zihuatanejo.com.mx/america/, $40–80) enjoy a tranquil, shady street location. The 10 two-bedroom kitchenette apartments, of various sizes, are stacked in two floors around an inner patio-corridor. They are plainly but comfortably furnished with tile floors, bedspreads, curtains, and well-maintained shower baths. They rent, low-season, for about $40, $60, or $80 per day ($600, $800, $1,000 per month) for up to four, six, or eight persons, respectively, with fans, hot water, modest café-restaurant out front, but no parking. Add $15/day for air-conditioning and 20 percent during the Christmas–Easter winter season. Choose an upstairs apartment for more light and air.

Fishing parties are steady customers at the **Hotel Hi-Sol** (Bravo 120, tel./fax 755/554-0595), three blocks from the beach. The hotel offers two floors of around a dozen spacious, clean, semideluxe rooms. All have shiny shower baths and are invitingly decorated with tile and cheery yellow-and-blue-motif bedspreads and curtains. All rooms open to airy, private street-view balconies. Rates run about $60 s or d, and $70 t or q low season and $80 s or d, $90 t, and $100 q high; with TV, fans, and telephone.

Hotel Ávila (Juan Álvarez 8, tel. 755/554-2010, $60 s or d), downtown Zihuatanejo's only beachfront hostelry, is popular for its location. Rooms, although simply decorated, are comfortable. Guests in the hotel's several beachfront rooms enjoy luxurious private-patio bay and beach views. If possible avoid taking a room on the noisy streetfront side. The 27 rooms rent for about $70 s or d with view and $60 without in the low season, $85 s or d with view, $75 without high. All rooms have fans, TV, air-conditioning, phones, and hot water. Credit cards are accepted.

PLAYA MADERA

Another sizable fraction of Zihuatanejo's lodgings spreads along and above Playa Madera on the east side of the bay, easily reachable in a few blocks on foot from the town plaza, via the scenic beachfront *andador* (walkway). Many of the lodgings are picturesquely perched along leafy Calle Eva Samano de López Mateos, which runs atop Cerro Madera, the bayfront hill just east of town, while others dot Avenida Adelita at the foot of Cerro Madera. Guests in all of the Playa Madera lodgings described here enjoy direct beach access by simply strolling a block or less downhill to luscious Playa Madera.

Note: Because of Zihuatanejo's one-way streets (which fortunately direct most noisy traffic away from downtown), getting to Cerro Madera by car is a bit tricky. The key is Plaza Kyoto, the traffic-circle intersection of Paseo de la Boquita and Paseo del Palmar a quarter mile east of downtown. Keep a sharp eye out and follow the small Zona Hotelera signs. At Plaza Kyoto, marked by a big Japanese *torii* gate, bear right across the canal bridge and turn right at the first street, Señora de los Remedios. Continue for another block to Avenida Adelita, address of several Playa Madera hotels, which runs along the base of Cerro Madera. At Adelita, continue straight uphill to the lane that runs atop Cerro Madera, Calle Eva Samano de López Mateos.

$50-100

Playa Madera's only beachfront low-end lodging is the 1960s-era **Bungalows Allec** (Calle Eva Samano de López Mateos, Cerro Madera, tel./fax 755/554-2002, reservarbuallec@bungalows allec.com, www.bungalowsallec.com). Comfortable, light, and spacious although somewhat worn, the 12 clean fan-only apartments have breezy bay views from private balconies. Six of the units are very large, with two bedrooms, sleeping at least four, and kitchenettes. The others are smaller studio doubles with refrigerator. No pool, but Playa Madera is half a block downhill. The kitchenette apartments go for about $110 low season, $180 high; the smaller studios run about $50 low, $75 high, with parking and credit cards accepted. Long-term discounts may be available.

A couple of blocks inland from the beach find the family-friendly **Bungalows El Milagro** (Av. Marina Nacional s/n, Playa Madera, tel. 755/554-3045, klausbuhrer@hotmail.com, www.ixtapa-zihuatanejo.net/elmilagro/, $65 d low season, $85 d high), the life project of Dr. Niklaus Bührer and his wife, Lucina Gomes. A haciendalike walled compound of cottages and apartments, clustered around a shady pool, Bungalows El Milagro is winter headquarters for a cordial group of longtimer German returnees. The welcoming atmosphere and the inviting pool and garden account for El Milagro's success, rather than the plain but clean kitchenette lodgings, which vary in style from rustic to 1950s Bavarian motel. Look at several before you choose. The 17 units rent low season (excepting high season Christmas through Easter and July and August) for about $65 d ($900/month) for the smaller to about $140 ($1,100/month) for the larger family-sized units. Add about 25 percent high season. All with fully furnished kitchenettes with purified water, hot water, fans, pool, and parking.

On Avenida Adelita, right above the beach, stands the longtime Mexican family–run **Hotel Palacio** (Av. Adelita, Playa Madera, tel./fax 755/554-2055, hotelpalacio@prodigy .net.mx, $65 d, $80 d high) a beachfront maze of rooms connected by meandering multilevel walkways. Room windows along the two main tiers face corridor walkways, where curtains must be drawn for privacy. Upper units fronting the quiet street avoid this drawback. The rooms themselves are clean, renovated, brightly decorated, and comfortable, with fans or air-conditioning and hot water. Guests enjoy a small but pleasant bayview pool, kiddie pool, and sundeck, which perches above the waves at the hotel beachfront. Low-season rentals run about $55 s, $65 d with fan, add $10 for air-conditioning, all with TV and hot water, but street parking only. Add about 20 percent high season.

Back atop Cerro Madera, **(Casa Azul** (tel. 755/554-3534, info@casaazul-zihuatanejo .com, www.casaazul-zihuatanejo.com, from $50 d lowest season, $115 Christmas holiday) offers a touch of luxury and restful ambience at moderate rates. Owner Marsha Gould rents three apartments, two uppers (*arriba*) and one lower (*abajo*). The larger upper (Casa Azul *arriba*) is a tropical hideaway for two, with a luxuriously rustic *palapa* roof, loft bedroom with king-sized bed, sleeping couch for one, and a private, airy bayview balcony. The other upper, El Nido (the nest), is romantic and cozy, with a rustic red-tile roof, double bed, and bayview balcony. The larger apartment *abajo* is equally comfortable, but darker, with two bedrooms sleeping up to six, living-dining room, and a town-view garden patio. All apartments have full kitchenettes and hot-water shower baths. The Casa Azul upper unit rents, double occupancy, for either $85, $95, or $115, depending on the season, the El Nido upper, similarly, for $70, $80, or $100, and the lower for $50, $60, $70, or $90; add $10 for each extra person. All accommodations are nonsmoking. Marsha leaves town June through October, although she does offer the downstairs apartment while she's gone.

Several apartment bungalow–style complexes cluster along the same scenic Cerro Madera hilltop street. Although their details differ, their basic layouts—which stair-step artfully downhill to private beachfront gardens—are similar. Typical among them is **Bungalows Sotelo** (Calle Eva Samano de López Mateos 13, tel./fax 755/554-6307, reservar@bungalows sotelo.com, www.bungalowssotelo.com, $70 d low, $90 high). Guests in a number of clean and comfortable stucco-and-tile apartments enjoy spacious private or semiprivate terraces with deck lounges and bay views. Rents for the smaller units without kitchenette run about $70 d low season, $90 high; larger kitchenette suites rent for about $85 d low season, $130 high (for one bedroom) and $100 low season, $150 high (for two bedrooms). Rentals vary; look at more than one before deciding. No pool, street parking only, but with air-conditioning; get your winter reservations in early.

Also atop Cerro Madera, consider the spiffy **(Bungalows Ley** (Calle Eva Samano de López Mateos s/n, Playa Madera, tel. 755/554-4087, fax 755/554-1365, bungalows ley@prodigy.net.mx). Here, several white-stucco studio apartments stair-step directly downhill to heavenly Playa Madera. Their recent decorations show nicely. Bathrooms shine with flowery Mexican tile, hammocks hang in spacious rustic-chic *palapa*-roofed view patios, and bedrooms glow with wall art, native wood details, and soothing pastel bedspreads. Except for a two-bedroom kitchenette unit at the top, all are kitchenette studios with air-conditioning and telephone. No pool, but the beach is straight down the steps from your door. The studios run about $70 d low season, $90 high. The beautiful two-bedroom unit also with air-conditioning runs $115 low season for up to four, $170 high. Long-term low-season discounts (of 15–30 percent for 6- to 21-night stays) are available.

Back downhill, the **(Hotel Villas Miramar** (Av. Adelita, Playa Madera, tel. 755/554-2106, toll-free Mex. tel. 01-800/570-6767, fax 755/554-2149, reservaciones@hotelvillas miramar.com, www.hotelvillasmiramar.com, $75 d low season, $130 high) clusters artfully around gardens of pools, palms, and leafy potted plants. The gorgeous, manicured layout makes maximum use of space, creating both privacy and intimacy in a small setting. The designer rooms have high ceilings, split levels, built-in sofas, and large, comfortable beds. The street divides the hotel into two different but lovely sections, each with its own pool. The restaurant, especially convenient for breakfast, is in the shoreside section but still serves guests who sun and snooze around the luxurious, beachview pool-patio on the other side of the street. The garden rooms rent for about $75 d low season, $130 high; the oceanview apartments about $95 d low, $150 high; all have phones, cable TV, and air-conditioning, some have wheelchair access. Credit cards are accepted. Additional discounts may be available during May–December 15 low season. Reservations strongly recommended during the high season.

Half a block east, overlooking the beach, **⟨ Hotel Irma** (Av. Adelita, Playa Madera, tel./fax 755/554-8003 or 755/554-8472, fax 755/554-3738, toll-free U.S./Can. tel. 800/262-4500, info@mcrx.com, www.hotel irma.com.mx, $90 d low, $100 high) remains a favorite of longtime lovers of Zihuatanejo, if for no reason other than its location. Guests enjoy very comfortable renovated deluxe rooms, a

good bayview terrace restaurant and bar, and a pair of blue pools perched above the bay. A short walk downhill and you're at creamy Madera beach. Best of all, many of the front-tier rooms have private balconies with just about the loveliest view on Playa Madera. The 70 rooms rent for about $100 s or d low season, $125 high, with view ($90 low and $100 high without view), all with air-conditioning, TV, hot water, and wireless Internet connection.

Over $100

One of the fanciest Cerro Madera options is the **Hotel Brisas del Mar** (Calle Eva Samano de López Mateos s/n, Cerro Madera, tel./fax 755/554-8332 or 755/554-2142, brisamar@prodigy.net.mx, info@hotelbrisasdelmar.com, www.hotelbrisasdelmar.com, $115 low, $134 high). Owners have completely renovated the original complex and have added a big new wing of a dozen spacious, rustic-chic view suites with native Mexico decor to the original 20 apartments. The brightest spot of this entire complex, besides its sweeping bay views, is the hotel's lovely beach club, with its shady *palapas,* lounge chairs, and big blue pool. For

© BRUCE WHIPPERMAN

Zihuatanejo Bay, from the Hotel Irma poolside

such amenities, Brisas del Mar asks premium prices. Its original (but upgraded) apartments rent for about $115 d low season, $134 high. Larger master suites go for $145 low, $184 high, while the spacious two-bedroom family bungalows, with kitchen, run $309 low, $370 high, all with oceanview patios, air-conditioning, and cable TV.

Also on Cerro Madera, perched atop Bungalows Ley, with the same address but completely separate, is upscale **〖 Casa Leigh y Loros** (Calle Eva Samano de López Mateos s/n, Playa Madera, tel. 755/554-3755, zihua01@ gmail.com, www.zihuatanejo-rentals.com, $155 low, $225 high), the lovely life project of friendly California resident Leigh Roth and her pet parrot, Loros. Casa Leigh y Loros, which Leigh rents when she's away, is a multilevel art-decorated white-stucco-and-tile two-bedroom, two-bath villa with roof garden, airy bayview balconies, and up-to-date kitchen appliances. High winter season (except Christmas) rent runs about $225 d, with fans, $255 with air-conditioning November 15–April 30, $155 and $180 May 1–November 14. All with cable TV and daily maid service; a cook is available at extra charge. Leigh also manages rentals for many other luxurious villas, apartments, and condominiums. See her website and/or contact Ignacio, her rental agent, in Zihuatanejo, at local cell tel. 044-755/559-8884.

A few hundred yards farther east along cliffside Paseo Costera toward Playa La Ropa, find **〖 La Casa Que Canta** (Camino Escénico a Playa La Ropa, tel. 755/555-7030, toll-free Mex. tel. 800/710-9345 or U.S. tel. 888/523-5050, fax 755/554-7900, info@lacasaquecanta.com, www.lacasaquecanta.com), which is as much a work of art as a hotel. The pageant begins at the lobby, a luxurious soaring *palapa* that angles gracefully down the cliffside to an intimate open-air view dining room. Suite clusters of natural adobe sheltered by thick *palapa* roofs cling artfully to the craggy precipice decorated with riots of bougainvillea and gardens of cactus. From petite pool terraces perched above foamy shoals, guests enjoy a radiant aqua bay panorama in the morning and brilliant ridge-silhouetted sunsets in the evening. The 18 art-bedecked, rustic-chic suites, all with private view balconies, come in three grades: super-deluxe "terrace" rooms, more spacious "grand suites," and even more spacious and luxurious "master suites," the latter two options with their own small pools. Year-round asking rates are $590, $700, and $990, respectively. All come with air-conditioning, fans, and phone, but no TV; no kids under 16 allowed. Make winter reservations very early.

(*Note:* Casa Que Canta now offers the best of all possible upscale worlds within its present grounds: the El Murmullo super-private 10,000-square-foot four-villa inner sanctum compound, built for a maharaja. It includes complete all-exclusive staff, from gardener, chambermaids, and butler to waiters, kitchen staff, and gourmet chef, all for only about $4,500 daily.)

PLAYA LA ROPA
$50-100

For Playa La Ropa's most moderately priced lodging, go nearly all the way to the end of the beach, to the **Hotel Casa del Mar** (Playa La Ropa, tel./fax 755/554-3873, reserv@zihua-casadelmar.com, www.zihua-casadelmar.com or www.zihuatanejo-rentals.com/casadelmar, $85 d, $95 high), founded by master scuba diver Juan Barnard Avila and his wife, Margo. In the mid-1990s, Juan and Margo renovated a rickety old hotel, cleaned up the adjacent mangrove lagoon, and nurtured its wildlife (dozens of bird species and a number of crocodiles) back to health. They added 14 units around a rear jungle-garden and pool-patio. Now, new owners carry on Juan and Margo's ecological mission, with a restful hotel and beachfront restaurant where guests may stay and relax for a week or a season, enjoy wholesome food, friendly folks, and sample the good snorkeling, scuba diving, kayaking, turtle hatching, and fishing available right from the beach. Choose a room with an ocean view in front, or a garden view in back. All rooms are immaculate and simply but comfortably furnished with handsomely handcrafted wooden beds, lamps, and cabinets. Low-season rentals with fan only run about $95 d with ocean view, $85 d with garden view; high season, $120 and $95. Add about $15 for air-conditioning; all with hot-water baths, parking, small tank pool, and credit cards accepted. Reservations are mandatory in winter.

Back at the Zihuatanejo end of the strand, **Beach Resort Sotavento** (Playa La Ropa 01 s/n, tel. 755/554-2032, toll-free U.S. tel. 877/699-6685 or Can. tel. 877/667-3702, fax 755/554-2975, info@beachresortsotavento .com, www.beachresortsotavento.com, credit cards accepted, $65–95 d low, $70–185 d high) marks the beginning of luscious Playa La Ropa. Competent hands-on management keeps the rambling 90-room complex, which perches on a leafy bayview hillside, healthy. The Sotavento is a 1960s mod-style warren that stair-steps five stories (with no elevator) down a jungly beachfront slope. Each floor of rooms extends outward to a broad, hammock-hung communal or semi-private terrace, some with unobstructed ocean views. Inside, the Sotavento's rooms are spartan, clean, and comfortable, many with king- or queen-sized beds and all with ceiling fans. Rates vary according to season; low season: Easter–mid-July and Nov.–Dec. 15, midseason: middle of July until middle of August, high season: Dec. 15–Easter. Accommodations, all including hot breakfast, come in four variations: large upper-level *terraza* suites, virtually all with ocean views, suitable for a couple up to a family of six ($75 low season, $95 midseason, $145 high season); mid-sized middle-level *playa* studios, some with ocean views, with two beds, for up to four ($65, $85, and $85); smaller beach level *oceano* rooms, shaded by the beachfront forest, very few ocean views, with two beds, for up to three ($65, $70, and $70) and deluxe top-of-the-line *capitán* suites for four or more ($95, $110, and $185). (*Note:* Views, light, and shade depend on a room's vertical position in the stack. Guests in upper rooms enjoy expansive bay and sunset vistas, while guests in less pricey lower-level rooms nevertheless enjoy intimate tropical verdure-framed sunset vistas of the bay beyond. Maybe look at both kinds of rooms before choosing.) The Sotavento's amenities include a beachside pool, room fans, parking, a restaurant, and a beach aquatics shop, but no elevator or wheelchair access.

Among the dozen-odd hotels, bungalow complexes, and restaurants that sprinkle the La Ropa beachfront is a trio of comfortable housekeeping bungalow complexes that share the same choice shoreline as the renowned Hotel Tides (described later), but offer lodging at much more modest rates.

One of these is ◖ **Bungalows Urracas** (Playa La Ropa, tel. 755/554-2053 in Spanish only), made up of about 15 petite brick cottages, like proper rubber planter's bungalows out of Somerset Maugham's *Malaysian Stories,* nestling in a shady jungle of leafy bushes, trees, and vines. Inside, the illusion continues: dark, masculine wood furniture, spacious bedrooms, shiny tiled kitchenettes and baths, and rustic beamed ceilings. From the bungalows, short garden paths lead to the brilliant La Ropa beachfront. About eight additional bungalows occupy beachview locations out front. Amenities include private shady front porches (use insect repellent in the evenings), hot-water baths, and fans. Rentals run a bargain $70 d low season, $80 high. Ask for a long-term discount. Telephone is their only communication option. Get your winter reservations in very early (if necessary, ask someone who speaks Spanish to call).

In contrast nearby is **Bungalows Vepao** (Playa La Ropa, tel. 755/554-3619, fax 755/554-5003, vepao@yahoo.com.mx, www .vepao.com, $75 d, $85 high). Here you can enjoy a clean, pleasantly tranquil beach lodging, simply but architecturally designed, with floor-to-ceiling drapes, modern-standard kitchenettes, tiled floors, hot-water shower baths, white stucco walls, and pastel bedspreads and shaded lamps. Guests in each of the six side-by side apartments enjoy front patios (upper ones have some bay view) that lead right to the hotel's private row of nearby beachfront thatched *palapas*. Rates include parking and fans; long-term discounts are possible. Reserve through owner-manager Verónica Ramírez, by fax or phone (in Spanish, 7 A.M.–6 P.M. Pacific Time).

Back near the Zihuatanejo end of the beach, a block off the beach, **Villas Ema** (Calle Delfines, reserve through the Posada Citlali, Av. Guerrero 3, downtown Zihuatanejo, tel./fax 755/554-2043, or in Spanish at the Villas tel. 755/554-4880, villasema@zihuatanejo .com.mx, $80 d, $110 high) perches at the top of a flowery hillside garden. Here, the enterprising husband-and-wife owners of downtown Posada Citlali have built about a dozen apartments, beautifully furnished with white tile floors, matching floral drapes and bedspreads, modern-standard shower baths, plenty of windows for light, and sliding doors leading to private view porches for reading and relaxing. Amenities include air-conditioning or fans, hot water, a beautiful blue pool, and the murmur of the waves on Playa La Ropa nearby. Rates for the nine smaller units, with a shared kitchen in common, run about $80 d low season, $110 high. The three top-level units, although sunnier (and consequently warmer), have the best views and most privacy. Two ground-level larger *villitas*, by the pool, each with its own kitchen and patio and sleeping four, rent for about $110 low season, $130 high. For reservations, highly recommended in winter, contact the owners through Posada Citlali. To avoid confusion, be sure to specify your reservation is for Villas Ema.

Over $100

On the beachfront, adjacent to Bungalows Vepao, also find **[** **Casa Gloria Maria** (Playa La Ropa, tel. 755/554-3510, gloriamaria@ zihuatanejo.net, www.zihuatanejo.net/casa gloriamaria, $100 d low, $120 high), a designer white-stucco beachfront house of four apartments. Each of the deluxe units (two upstairs and two down) is attractively decorated with native rustic tile floors, bright floral tile baths, and whimsical hand-painted wall designs at the head of the two queen-sized beds. Each unit has its own kitchenette in an outdoor beach-view patio. For more breeze and privacy, ask for

one of the top-floor units. Rentals run about $100 low season, $120 high, with air-conditioning, hot-water baths, and parking.

Back toward Zihuatanejo, near the beginning of the beach, the **Hotel Villa Mexicana** (Playa La Ropa, tel./fax 755/554-3776, 755/554-3636, or 755/554-1331, www.villa mexicana.com.mx, from $90 d) seems to be popular for nothing more than its stunning location right in the middle of the sunny beach hubbub. Its 75 rooms, comfortable and air-conditioned, are packed in low-rise stucco clusters around an inviting beachfront pool-patio-restaurant. This seems just perfect for the mostly North American winter package-vacation clientele, who ride personal watercraft, parasail, and boogie board from the beach, snooze around the pool, and socialize beneath the *palapa* of the beachside restaurant. Low-season rates begin at about $90 d, and rise to a maximum of about $230 d around Christmas. Low-season three-night packages typically run about $250 d, including breakfast. Some rooms have wheelchair access. Parking is available; credit cards are accepted. Rooms can be reserved directly through the hotel or with the agency Mexico Hotel and Condo Reservations (toll-free U.S./Can. tel. 800/262-4500, info@ mcrx.com or reservations@mcrx.com, www .mexicocondores.com/zihuatanejo).

By contrast, the 40-odd lodgings of the hillside **[** **Catalina Beach Resort** (tel. 755/554-2137 or 755/554-9321 through 755/554-9325, toll-free U.S. tel. 877/287-2411 or Can. tel. 866/485-4312, fax 755/554-9327, info@catalinabeachresort.com, www.catalina beachresort.com), next to the Beach Resort Sotavento, stair-step picturesquely all the way down to the beach. The Catalina's comfortably appointed, 1960s-era tropical-rustic accommodations maximize privacy, with individual view terraces and hammocks. The spacious lodgings, all clean and deluxe, vary from large to huge; look until you find the one that most suits you. Most have fans only (not necessarily a minus on this airy hillside); some do have air-conditioning, however. At the bottom of the hill, a beach aquatics shop offers sailing, sailboarding, snorkeling, and other rentals; those who want to simply rest enjoy chairs beneath the shady boughs of a beachside grove. The Catalina's food and drink facilities include a view restaurant, perching in the middle of the complex, a snack bar down at the beach, and an airy upper-level terrace bar. Access to all of this requires lots of stair climbing, which fitness aficionados would consider a plus. The Catalina's high-season rates for two run as follows: small casita (large room) $120 fan only; standard casita (suite) $150 fan only; deluxe bungalow (even larger suite) $187 with air-conditioning; deluxe honeymoon suite with air-conditioning $219; all with cable TV and phone. Low-season rates for the same categories run about $88, $116, $130, and $134.

German entrepreneur Helmut Leins left Munich and came to create paradise on Playa La Ropa in 1978. The result was Playa La Ropa's renowned Villa del Sol, now being operated by new owners as the **Hotel Tides Zihuatanejo** (Playa La Ropa, tel. 755/555-5500, toll-free U.S./Can. tel. 866/905-9560, fax 755/554-2758, reservations@tideszihuatanejo .com, www.tideszihuatanejo.com). Here, in an exquisite beachside mini-Eden, a corps of well-to-do North American, European, and Mexican clients return yearly to enjoy tranquillity and the elegance of Tides Zihuatanejo's crystal-blue pools, palm-draped patios, and gourmet *palapa*-shaded restaurants. The lodgings vary, from luxuriously spacious at the high end to simply large at the low end; all have handsome rustic floor tile, handcrafted wall art, and big, luxuriously soft beds. The plethora of extras includes restaurants, bars, pools, night tennis courts, a newsstand, art gallery boutique, beauty salon, and meeting rooms. The least expensive of the approximately 70 accommodations begins at $330 s or d low season, $500 high. Super-plush room options include more bedrooms and baths, ocean views, and small private whirlpool tubs for around $800 and up. All lodgings come with cable TV, phone, air-conditioning, and parking; some have wheelchair access. Credit cards are accepted, but children are permitted in two-bedroom suites only.

IXTAPA

Ixtapa's dozen-odd hotels line up in a luxurious strip between the beach and boulevard Paseo Ixtapa. Guests in all of them enjoy deluxe resort-style facilities and wheelchair access. All are high-end (more than $100/day) accommodations.

Near the northwest end, consider the best-buy Spanish-owned ◖ **Hotel NH Krystal Ixtapa** (Paseo Ixtapa s/n, tel. 755/553-0333, toll-free U.S. tel. 888/726-0528 or Can. tel. 866/299-7096, fax 755/553-0216, nhixtapa@nh-hoteles.com.mx, www.nh-hoteles .com, as little as $113 d low, $314 high). The hotel, which towers over its spacious garden compound, has an innovative wedge design that ensures an ocean view from each room. Relaxation centers on the blue pool, where guests enjoy watching each other slip from the water slide and duck beneath the waterfall all day. Upstairs, all of the 260 tastefully appointed deluxe rooms and suites have private view balconies, cable TV, air-conditioning, and phones. Check for additional discounts through extended-stay or other packages. Extras include tennis courts, racquetball, an exercise gym, and parking. Credit cards are accepted.

Another good-value choice is the Best Western **Hotel Posada Real** (Paseo Ixtapa s/n, tel. 755/553-1625 or 755/553-1745, Best Western toll-free U.S./Can. tel. 800/528-1234, fax 755/553-1805, ixtapa@posadareal.com .mx, www.bestwestern.com or www.posada real.com.mx, $135 d low, $230 high), at Paseo Ixtapa's northwest end. Get there via the street, beach side, just past the big corner restaurant on the left. With a large grassy soccer field instead of tennis courts, the hotel attracts a seasonal following of soccer enthusiasts. Other amenities include a large airy beachfront restaurant and two luscious pools. Although the 110 (rather small) rooms are clean and comfortable, many lack ocean views. Extended-stay or low-season discounts, such as a third night free, are often available. Kids under 12 stay free with parents. Amenities include air-conditioning, satellite TV, phones, and parking; credit cards are accepted.

Right in the middle of the hotel zone stands

© BRUCE WHIPPERMAN

The Hotel NH Krystal is one of Ixtapa's best-buy luxury hotels.

the **Hotel Dorado Pacífico** (Paseo Ixtapa s/n, tel. 755/553-2025, fax 755/553-0126, reserv@doradopacifico.com.mx, www.doradopacifico.com.mx, $175 d low, $250 high). Here, three palm-shaded blue pools, water slides, a swim-up bar, and three restaurant-bars continue to satisfy a year-round crowd of vacationers. Upstairs, the rooms, all with sea-view balconies, are pleasingly decorated with sky-blue carpets and earth-tone designer bedspreads. The 285 rooms have air-conditioning, phones, and cable TV. Low-season and extended-stay discounts may be available. Other extras include tennis courts and parking; credit cards are accepted.

At the east end, **Hotel Barceló Ixtapa Beach** (Paseo Ixtapa s/n, tel. 755/555-2000, toll-free U.S. tel. 800/227-2356, fax 755/553-2438, reservas@barceloixtapa.com or ixtapa@barcelo.com, www.barceloixtapa.com), across from the golf course at the east end of the beach, rises around a soaring lobby/atrium. The Barceló, formerly the Sheraton, offers a long list of resort facilities, including pools, all sports, an exercise gym, several restaurants and bars, cooking and arts lessons, nightly dancing, and a Fiesta Mexicana show-buffet. The 330-odd rooms in standard (which include inland-view balconies only), oceanview, and junior suite grades, are spacious and tastefully furnished in designer pastels and include air-conditioning, phones, and satellite TV. The Barceló offers only all-inclusive lodging. Rates (with all drinks, food, and entertainment included) are about $195 per person, double occupancy low season, $300 d high, kids under six free, 6–12 $60.

From its east-end jungly hilltop perch, the queen of Ixtapa hotels, the ◖ **Hotel Las Brisas Ixtapa** (Paseo de la Roca, tel. 755/553-2121, toll-free Mex. tel. 800/227-4727 or U.S./Can. tel. 888/559-4329, fax 755/553-1038, ixtapa@brisas.com.mx, www.brisas.com.mx) slopes downhill to the shore like a latter-day Aztec pyramid. The monumentally stark hilltop lobby, open and unadorned except for a clutch of huge stone balls, contrasts sharply with its surroundings. The hotel's severe lines immediately shift the focus to the adjacent jungle. The fecund forest aroma wafts into the lobby and the terrace restaurant where, at breakfast during the winter and early spring, guests sit watching iguanas munch hibiscus blossoms in the nearby treetops. The hotel entertains guests with a wealth of luxurious resort facilities, including pools, four tennis courts, a gym, aerobics, an intimate shoal-enfolded beach, restaurants, bars, and

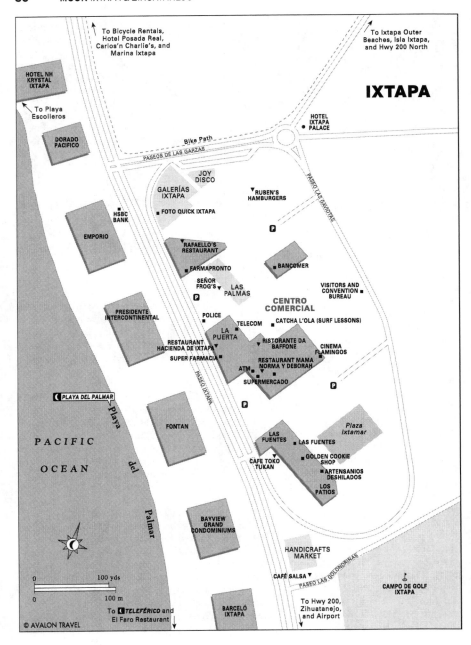

IXTAPA

To Bicycle Rentals,
Hotel Posada Real,
Carlos'n Charlie's, and
Marina Ixtapa

To Ixtapa Outer
Beaches, Isla Ixtapa,
and Hwy 200 North

HOTEL NH
KRYSTAL
IXTAPA

To Playa
Escolleros

DORADO
PACIFICO

HOTEL
IXTAPA
PALACE

Bike Path

PASEOS DE LAS GARZAS

PASEO LAS GAVIOTAS

JOY
DISCO

GALERÍAS
IXTAPA

RUBEN'S
HAMBURGERS

HSBC
BANK

FOTO QUICK IXTAPA

EMPORIO

Rafaello's
RESTAURANT

FARMAPRONTO

BANCOMER

SEÑOR
FROG'S

LAS
PALMAS

VISITORS AND
CONVENTION
BUREAU

CENTRO
COMERCIAL

PRESIDENTE
INTERCONTINENTAL

POLICE

TELECOM

CATCHA L'OLA (SURF LESSONS)

LA
PUERTA

RESTAURANT
HACIENDA DE IXTAPA

RISTORANTE DA
BAFFONE

CINEMA
FLAMINGOS

SUPER FARMACIA

RESTAURANT MAMA
NORMA Y DEBORAH

ATM

SUPERMERCADO

PLAYA DEL PALMAR

Playa del Palmar

PACIFIC

OCEAN

FONTAN

Plaza
Ixtamar

LAS
FUENTES

LAS FUENTES

GOLDEN COOKIE
SHOP

CAFE TOKO
TUKAN

ARTENSANIOS
DESHILADOS

LOS
PATIOS

PASEO IXTAPA

BAYVIEW
GRAND
CONDOMINIUMS

HANDICRAFTS
MARKET

CAFÉ SALSA

PASEO LAS GOLONDRINAS

CAMPO DE GOLF
IXTAPA

0   100 yds

0   100 m

To TELEFÉRICO and
El Faro Restaurant

BARCELÓ
IXTAPA

To Hwy 200,
Zihuatanejo,
and Airport

© AVALON TRAVEL

Hotel Las Brisas Ixtapa

nightly piano-bar music. The standard rooms, each with its own spacious view patio, are luxuriously spartan, floored with big designer tiles, furnished in earth tones, and equipped with big TVs, small refrigerators, phones, and air-conditioning. More luxurious options include suites with individual pools and hot tubs. The 427 rooms begin at about $250 for a standard low-season double, $540 high, and run about twice that for super-luxury suites. June–October, bargain packages can push standard-room prices as low as $150 d.

PLAYA LINDA

A trio of all-inclusive luxury resort hotels decorate the luscious, tranquil Playa Linda beachfront about five miles (8 km) northwest of the main Ixtapa hotel zone.

The original of the three is the **Club Med Ixtapa** (toll-free U.S. tel. 800/258-2633, www.clubmed.com), which, as its long-time clients have acquired families, has become kid friendly. Besides deluxe rooms, the usual good Club Med food, and a plethora of included activities,

from sailboating and surfing to water aerobics and chess, children can also enjoy a full supervised program of child-appropriate activities. At Club Med, the usual lodging arrangement is for a minimum of one week, paid in advance. Typical winter (non-holiday) weekly rates run about $1,500 per adult, about $1,100 summer–fall low season, with discounts for kids.

Alternatively, you could consider the Club Med's worthy neighbors, the **Hotel Meliá Azul Ixtapa** (tel. 755/555-0000, toll-free U.S./ Can. tel. 800/336-3542, fax 755/555-0100, www.meliaazulixtapa.solmelia.com), and the **Hotel Qualton Club** (tel. 755/552-0080, www.qualton.com/ixtapa). They both welcome children and offer deluxe amenities, food, and activities comparable to Club Med, often at reduced prices.

TRAILER PARKS AND CAMPING

The Ixtapa and Zihuatanejo area has two equipped RV-camping parks, one small, on Playa Ropa in Zihuatanejo, and one large government-built site, on Ixtapa's far outer beach, Playa Larga. Two other small rough work-in-progress sites offer some RV hookups and camping space on Playa La Ropa. Get your winter reservations in months in advance. (The former homey Trailer Park Las Cabañas on Playa la Ropa has closed.)

Although at this writing the government-run Playa Larga RV park, officially **Ixtapa Trailer Park** (Lote 36, Real Playa Larga, tel. 755/552-0295 or 755/552-0296, trailerpark ixtapa@gmail.com, $25 low, $30 high, camping $7 per person), is still being finished, basic facilities—including high-power electricity, water, drainage, showers, toilets, and a restaurant—have been installed. The site, right by breezy, palm-shadowed Playa Larga, fine for all beach pastimes, is promising. Presently, they offer about 50 unshaded asphalt RV spaces (big enough for 35-foot rigs) inside their cyclone fence, about five miles (8 km) from Ixtapa, ten miles (16 km) to Zihuatanejo. Get there by driving to Playa Linda (see *Ixtapa Outer Beaches*. Continue north (follow RV park signs), past the Playa Linda bridge and parking lot, continuing about another half-mile to the RV park on the left.

A much smaller and informal spot to park your RV or put up a tent is at the far end of Playa La Ropa: **El Manglar Restaurant and RV Park** (Playa La Ropa, tel. 755/554-3752, $20 per RV, $10 for tent), on the inland side of the mangrove lagoon adjacent to the beachfront Hotel Casa del Mar. Here, the friendly restaurant owners who also run the trailer park offer parking space for about ten RVs, with all hookups, clean showers, and resident lagoon crocodiles (watch your toddlers and pets). Pluses here are a good restaurant, two-minute walk to lovely Playa la Ropa, space for about five large rigs and five small, and a locked gate at night. Minuses are lack of shade and evening no-see-ums and mosquitoes. To get to El Manglar, first follow the directions under *Playa Madera* earlier in the *Accommodations* section. Past Plaza Kyoto and the canal bridge, instead of turning right on Señora de los Remedios street, continue straight ahead two blocks. Pass the Bungalows El Milagro on the right, climb the hill for half a block and bear right for a long block, then turn left where the street forks, and you'll be on your way, with a fine bay view, along Paseo Costera. Continue about a mile, winding toward Playa La Ropa. Downhill, continue straight ahead past a traffic circle and monument on the right. Continue another mile straight ahead, passing Hotel Real de Palma on the left. After about three blocks, turn right, to the signed El Manglar gate.

If the above two RV parks are full, you might find an RV parking space and/or campsite at either of a pair of rough possibilities: **Playa La Ropa Camping and RV** (near the middle of Playa La Ropa, see Esta Campamento signpost, $15), with several spaces with all hookups, and **Costa Bella** (tel. 755/554-4967), with a few unshaded hookups and camping spaces, also for about $15; right by the beach (pass under the arch) at the far south end of the Playa La Ropa road. (For more information and photos of all of the above trailer parks and camping possibilities, visit www.ontheroadin.com/pacific coast/pacificsouth/ixtapaandzihuat.htm).

RENTALS

Zihuatanejo residents sometimes offer their condos and homes for rent or lease through agents. Among the most experienced and highly recommended agents is **Judith Whitehead** (tel. 755/554-6226, cell tel. 044-755/557-0078, fax 755/553-1212, jude@prodigy.net.mx, www .paradise-properties.com.mx).

Also, owner-agent **Francisco Ibarra** (tel. 755/554-4924 or 755/554-9377, donfranciscoproperties@gmail.com, www.donfrancisco properties.com) rents several moderately priced condos and houses on Playa La Ropa.

For many more vacation rentals, visit the excellent websites www.zihuatanejo.net and www.zihuatanejo-rentals.com.

For modestly priced rentals, don't forget the **Hotel Monarca, Casa de Huéspedes Ada, Apartments America,** and **Hotel Amueblados Valle** in the *Downtown Zihuatanejo* section.

Food

ZIHUATANEJO
Snacks, Bakeries, and Breakfasts

For something cool in Zihuatanejo, stop by the **Paletería y Nevería Michoacana** (Álvarez, no phone, 9 A.M.–9 P.M. daily) ice shop across from the police station by the beachfront town plaza. Besides ice cream, popcorn, and safe *nieves* (ices), it offers delicious *aguas* (fruit-flavored drinks) that make nourishing, refreshing Pepsi-free alternatives.

All roads seem to lead to the excellent downtown Zihuatanejo bakery (**Buen Gusto** (Guerrero 11, 8 A.M.–10 P.M. daily, pastries about $0.30–0.80 each), on the east side of the street a few doors up from the restaurant Coconuts. Choose from a simply delicious assortment of fruit and nut tarts and cakes—pineapple, coconut, peach, strawberry, pecan—with good coffee to go with them all.

For hot sandwiches and good pizza on the downtown beach, try the **Cafe Marina** (tel. 755/554-2462, 8 A.M.–9 P.M. Mon.–Sat., closed approx. June to mid-Sept., $8), on Paseo del Pescador just west of the plaza. The friendly, hardworking owner features specials, such as spaghetti and meatballs, or ribs and potato salad, on some weeknights. The shelves of books for lending or exchange are nearly as popular as the food.

Playa Madera's prime breakfast spot is family-run **La Casa Cafe** (Av. Adelita 7, tel. 755/554-3467, 8 A.M.–1 P.M. Tues.–Sun., closed Sept. and Oct., $3–6), at the bottom of Cerro Madera, west end. Dad, mom, and the kids serve up a steady stream of bountiful omelettes, pancakes, breakfast burritos, fruit, tamales, sausage, ham, and fried potatoes to a legion of loyal customers.

A local vacation wouldn't be complete without dropping in at the **Sirena Gorda** (Fat Mermaid, tel. 755/554-2687, 9 A.M.–11 P.M. Thurs.–Tues., $4–9), near the end of Paseo del Pescador across from the naval compound. Here the fishing crowd relaxes, trading stories after a tough day hauling in the lines. The other unique attractions, besides the well-endowed sea nymphs who decorate the walls, are tempting shrimp-bacon and fish tacos, juicy hamburgers, fish *mole,* and conch and *nopal* (cactus leaves, minus the spines) plates.

On at least one Zihuatanejo day, be sure to enjoy breakfast at newcomer **❮ Restaurant Margarita** (on Guerrero a block from the beach, tel. 755/554-8380, 8 A.M.–11 P.M. daily, breakfast $2–3, lunch $6, dinner $7–10), across the street from the restaurant Coconuts. Besides a pleasantly refined old-world ambience including rustic beamed ceilings and soft music, they offer tasty, light entrées and attentive service. For example, for breakfast, choose an omelette or simply scrumptious *panes dulces* (pastries) along with your cappuccino and fresh-squeezed orange juice. For lunch, go for a tuna salad or *chiles*

rellenos; for supper try one of their excellent seafood entrées.

Restaurants

Local chefs and restaurateurs, long accustomed to foreign tastes, operate a number of good local restaurants, mostly in Zihuatanejo (where, in contrast to Ixtapa, most of the serious eating occurs *outside* of hotel dining rooms). Note, however, that a number of the best restaurants are closed during the low-season months of September and October. If in doubt, be sure to call ahead. The recommendations here move across downtown, generally from east to west.

Local folks swear by **❮ Cocina Económica Doña Licha** (Calle Cocos, tel. 755/554-3933, 7 A.M.–11 P.M. daily, $3–9) in downtown Zihuatanejo's northeast neighborhood. (From Plaza Kyoto, follow Palmera west one block, turn left onto Cocos and continue half a block.) The reason is clear: tasty local-style food, served promptly in an airy, spic-and-span setting. Here customers can have it all. For breakfast try *huevos a la Mexicana* or pancakes; for *lonche,* go for the four-course *comida corrida* set lunch; for *cena* (supper), try one of their super-fresh fish fillets or a seafood brochette (shrimp, oysters, octopus, fish).

All expatriate trails seem to lead eventually to **Restaurant Glob's** (corner of Juárez and Ejido, tel. 755/554-5727, 8 A.M.–10 P.M. daily year-round, $4–8), on the east side of downtown three blocks from the beach. Here the cool coffee-shop atmosphere is refined but friendly, and the food is strictly for comfort—good American breakfasts, hamburgers, spaghetti, and salads.

Zihuatanejo has a pair of good, genuinely Mexican-style restaurants, frequented by a legion of Zihuatanejo longtimers. In the central downtown area, **❮ Tamales y Atoles "Any"** (corner of Guerrero and Ejido, tel. 755/554-7373, 9 A.M.–11 P.M. daily, $4–8), arguably Zihuatanejo's best, is the spot to find out if your favorite Mexican restaurant back home is serving the real thing. Tacos, tamales, quesadillas, enchiladas, *chiles rellenos,* and such goodies are called *antojitos* in Mexico. At

Tamales y Atoles "Any," they're savory enough to please even demanding Mexican palates. Incidentally, Any (AH-nee) is the co-owner, whose perch is behind the cash register, while her friendly husband cooks and tends the tables.

Restaurant Los Braseros (Ejido 21, tel. 755/554-8736, 4 P.M.–1 A.M. daily, $3–5), half a block farther west along Ejido, between Cuauhtémoc and Guerrero, is similarly authentic and popular. Waiters are often busy after midnight even during low season serving seven kinds of tacos and specialties such as Gringa, Porky, and Azteca, from a menu it would take three months of dinners (followed by a six-month diet) to fully investigate.

One visit and you'll wish that Zihuatanejo had more restaurants like **Ⓒ Don Memo's** (Pedro Ascencio, local cell tel. 044-755/559-7000, 4:30–11:30 P.M. daily, $3.50–6), in the center of town a block from the beach. Here, you can enjoy a bountiful menu of no-nonsense Italian-Mexican specialties, accent on the Italian, but at Mexican prices. Tasty salads, piquant chicken chipotle, savory mushroom-tomato lasagna, tangy pulled pork smothered in tomatillo-chile *morita* sauce, and mushroom calzone: Bellisimo!

Asian-food fanciers have a choice of two good options. First, consider the very tasty offerings of Chinese restaurant **Mi Chayita** (Ejido, south side, recessed 100 feet off the street, betw. Guerrero and Galeana, tel. 755/554-5799, 11 A.M.–9 P.M. Mon.–Sat., $4–8) beneath its shady *palapa*. Here, a California-trained chef satisfies vegetable-hungry appetites, starting with bountifully delicious plates of chow mein and chop suey. On the other hand, meat eaters can choose from a list of many delicious favorites, such as sweet-and-sour pork, breaded shrimp, whole fish, broccoli beef, and much more.

For another Asian option, try **Esthela's Cocina and Express** (Cuauhtémoc betw. Ejido and Bravo, tel. 755/554-0352, 2–9 P.M. Tues.–Sun., $3–5), where local chef and Phillipine-American resident Esthela Buenaventura has relocated her popular longtime enterprise. She continues to offer her uniquely personal menu,

but now in an over-the-counter format (plastic utensils and bowls only), for either take-out or a few sit-down diners. Her tasty entrées consist of variations of stir-fried vegetables, to which she can add meat or fish for an additional price at your choice. For starters, Esthela offers such goodies as *lumpia* (Philippine-style spring rolls), cucumber salad, Buddha's Delight, and much more.

Up the street one block, families fill the tables at petite **Cocina Económica Carol** (Cuauhtémoc betw. Ejido and Gonzales, 11 A.M.–9 P.M. Mon.–Sat., $2–4). Diners enjoy country-style breakfasts such as *chilaquiles* and *huevos a la Mexicana*; *comida corrida* (set lunch of soup, rice, meat entrée, and dessert); and supper of tacos, enchiladas, tostadas, and tamales.

Down at the beach by the naval compound, longtime **Casa Elvira** (Paseo del Pescador, tel. 755/554-2061, 2–10 P.M. daily, $4–12), founded long ago by now-octogenarian Elvira Campos, is as popular as ever, still satisfying the palates of a battalion of loyal Zihuatanejo returnees. Elvira's continuing popularity is easy to explain: a palm-studded beachfront, strumming guitars, whirling ceiling fans, and a bounty of super-fresh salads and soups, hearty fish, meat and chicken entrées, and Mexican specialties, all expertly prepared and professionally served. Reservations recommended during the high season.

If Elvira's is full, an excellent seafood alternative would be **Porto de Mare** (tel. 755/554-5902, noon–11 P.M. daily, closed Sept.–Oct., $8–20) also on the beach, half a block east. It's the labor of love of its Italian architect owner, who designed and crafted its elegant open-air interior himself. As would be expected, his specialties are Italian-style pastas blended with superbly fresh local fish, shrimp, clams, scallops, and oysters.

No guide to Zihuatanejo restaurants would be complete without mention of **Ⓒ Coconuts** (on Guerrero a block from the beach, tel. 755/554-2518, noon–3:30 P.M. daily for Mexican *comida*, regular menu 6 P.M.–midnight daily in season, closed approx. July–Oct., $12–24). Here, the food—whether it be light (pasta primavera) or hearty (rib-eye steak)—appears to be of importance equal to the airy garden setting and good cheer generated among the droves of Zihuatanejo lovers who return year after year.

The owners of up-and-coming **Restaurant Capricio** (on Cinco de Mayo by the church, tel. 755/554-3019, 11 A.M.–11 P.M. daily, $8–20), on the southwest corner of downtown, have followed the successful Coconuts example. Soft background jazz, fairy lights, and a tropical greenery-festooned patio set the scene, while the cuisine of especially good seafood pastas, hamburgers, and steaks provides the main event.

Splurge Restaurants

Restaurant Kau Kan (tel. 755/554-8446, 5 P.M.–midnight daily, $16–30), on the clifftop road east and above Playa Madera, continues to be popular for both its romantic view location and its excellent food and service. While music plays softly and bay breezes gently blow, waiters scurry, bringing savory appetizers, Caesar salad, and cooked-to-perfection *dorado*, lobster, steak, and shrimp. High-season reservations mandatory.

Right next door and at least as worthy is Mediterranean boutique **☾ Restaurant Il Mare** (tel. 755/554-9067, noon–midnight daily high season, 4 P.M.–midnight daily low season, $20). Enter and let the luscious ambience—soothing Italian arias, waves crashing against the rocks far below, the golden setting sun—transport you somewhere on the southern Amalfi coast: *O! Sole mio!* The menu extends the impression: Start with *bruschetta alla Romagna*; follow with soup *brodetta di pesce*; salad *pomodoro cipolla rossa con gorgonzola*; and *scampi al vino bianco*, accompanied by a bottle of good Chilean Sendero chardonnay. Finish off with lemon liqueur *Sogna di Sorrento*. Reservations strongly recommended on weekends and in high season.

For a nouvelle variation, head downhill to Avenida Adelita (foot of Cerro Madera) and sample the "fusion" cuisine of hot new **Restaurant La Guia** (tel. 755/554-8396, 5:30–11 P.M. Mon.–Sat., closed Aug.–Oct., $12–30) Here, chefs practice the craft of small portions and

artful presentations of seafood (clams, lobster, shrimp, scallops) and pastas, steaks, and fowl. Reservations strongly recommended.

IXTAPA
Bakeries and Breakfasts

The perfume wafting from freshly baked European-style yummies draws dozens of the faithful to the **Golden Cookie Shop** (tel. 755/553-0310, 8 A.M.–2:30 P.M. Mon.–Fri., 8 A.M.–1 P.M. Sat., closed approx. July–Sept., $4–6), brainchild of local longtimers Helmut and his late wife, Esther Walter. On the inner patio, upper floor of Los Patios shopping complex, Helmut continues their mission of satisfying homesick palates with a continuous supply of scrumptious cinnamon rolls, pies, and hot buns, and hearty American-style breakfasts daily. In recent years, Helmut has served an authentic German buffet ($10) every Friday; call to confirm.

Alternatively, sample the good coffee and baked offerings of **Pan Nuestro** (Our Bread, in the Hotel Palacio Ixtapa, tel. 755/553-1585, 7 A.M.–midnight daily for pastries, 1 P.M.–midnight daily for pizza), at the north end of the Ixtapa shopping and restaurant complex, one block inland from the main boulevard.

Restaurants

Restaurants in Ixtapa have to be exceptional to compete with the hotels. One such, the **Bella Vista** (tel. 755/553-2121, 7 A.M.–11 P.M. daily, breakfast buffet $12, lunch $6–12, dinner $10–20), *is* in a hotel, being the Las Brisas Ixtapa's view-terrace café. Breakfast is the favorite time to watch the antics of the iguanas in the adjacent jungle treetops. These black, green, and white miniature dinosaurs crawl up and down the trunks, munch flowers, and sunbathe on the branches. The food and service, incidentally, are exceptional. Breakfast only in low season. Call ahead to reserve a terrace-edge table; credit cards are accepted.

The latter-day Ixtapa visitor flood has resulted in more recommendable Ixtapa restaurants. Favorite Zihuatanejo eateries have added Ixtapa branches, notably **Tamales y Atoles**

"Any" (on the north edge of La Puerta shopping complex, behind Restaurant Mama Norma and Deborah, tel. 755/553-3370, 8 A.M.–8 P.M. daily); see the listing under *Restaurants* in the preceding *Zihuatanejo* section.

Ruben's (tel. 755/553-0027, 8 A.M.–midnight daily, $3–5) hamburger and taco hall, at the north end of the Ixtapa Centro Comercial shopping complex, behind the corner Galerias Ixtapa center about a block inland from boulevard Paseo Ixtapa, is by far Ixtapa's most popular eatery, especially with the new flocks of Mexican vacationers. Ruben's is a phenomenon as much as it is a restaurant, outdoing traditional *taquerías* (taco stalls) at their own game, with fresh ingredients and snappy service by a squadron of or any of a dozen variations of steaks, hamburgers, and tacos.

An Ixtapa restaurant that has customers when most others don't is ● **Restaurant Mama Norma and Deborah** (tel. 755/553-0274, 7:30 A.M.–11 P.M. daily, $12–25), in the rear of La Puerta shopping center near Ristorante Da Baffone. Canadian expatriate proprietor Deborah Thompson manages with aplomb, working from a menu of delicious specialties familiar to North American and European palates. Whatever your choice, be it Greek salad, lobster, steak, or fettuccine Alfredo, Deborah makes sure it pleases. Lately she's been open for breakfast; call to confirm morning hours.

Folks hankering for Italian-style pastas and seafood walk next door to ● **Ristorante Da Baffone** (tel. 755/553-1122, 4 P.M. until about midnight daily, $10–12). The friendly owner, a native of the Italian isle of Sardinia, claims his restaurant is the oldest in Ixtapa. He's most likely right: He served his first meal here in 1978, simultaneous with the opening of Ixtapa's first hotel. While Mediterranean-Mex decor covers the walls, marinara-style shrimp, calamari, clams with linguini, ricotta- and spinach-stuffed cannelloni, and glasses of Chianti and *pino grigio* load the tables. Call to confirm hours and for reservations.

If Da Baffone is full or closed, or for a splurge, try the highly recommended Italian gourmet restaurant **Becco Fino** (tel. 755/553-1770, 9 A.M.–11 P.M. daily) in the Marina Ixtapa. Reservations are usually necessary. Figure spending at least $30 per person for dinner.

(Other Ixtapa restaurants, popular for their party atmosphere, are described in the following *Entertainment and Events* section.)

Entertainment and Events

In Zihuatanejo, visitors and residents content themselves mostly with quiet pleasures. Afternoons, they stroll the beachfront or the downtown shady lanes and enjoy coffee or drinks with friends at small cafés and bars. As the sun goes down, however, folks head to Ixtapa for its sunset vistas, happy hours, shows, clubs, and dancing.

NIGHTLIFE

Nightlife lovers are blessed with a broad range of enjoyable choices, sprinkled around Ixtapa and Zihuatanejo. In Ixtapa, options vary from the zany Carlos and Charlie's to the relaxed piano bar at El Faro restaurant. Zihuatanejo choices run from raucous Restaurant Bandidos to restful Restaurant Coconuts lounge bar.

Clubs and bars in Ixtapa are spread along main boulevard Paseo del Paseo del Palmar, and have the highest-volume, latest night options. Most of the Zihuatanejo choices are downtown (and usually close before midnight) and can be best discovered on a nighttime stroll while looking and listening for what you want.

Beginning in **Ixtapa,** high on the list is the part restaurant and part wacky seasonal nightspot **Carlos 'n Charlie's** (tel. 755/553-0085). It's as wild and as much fun as all of the other Carlos Anderson restaurants from Puerto

Vallarta to Paris. Here, you can have your picture taken on a surfboard in front of a big wave for $3, or have a helmeted firefighter spray out the flames from the chili sauce on your plate. Loud recorded rock music ($10 minimum) goes on 10 P.M.–4 A.M. during the winter season. The restaurant serves daily noon–midnight. Find it on the beachfront about half a block on the driveway road west past the Hotel Posada Real.

For more of the same, but even more loud and outrageous, go to **Señor Frog's** (tel. 755/553-2282), in the Ixtapa shopping plaza across from the Hotel Presidente Intercontinental.

Other Ixtapa choices include **Liquid** (behind Rafaello's restaurant, at the north end of the Ixtapa Commercial Center, opens about midnight, cover $10), a late-night cocktail bar with a DJ spinning techno-rock-progressive music, and the blues saxophonist at **El Faro** (tel. 755/553-2525, 8–11 P.M. Tues.–Sun.) restaurant, atop the lighthouse in Marina Ixtapa.

Continuing to **Zihuatanejo** downtown, check out open-air **Restaurant Bandidos** (tel. 755/553-8072, 10 P.M.–4 A.M. nightly high season), on Cinco de Mayo near the church, colorfully decorated in faux 1910 revolution style, with plenty of old Pancho Villa and Emiliano Zapata *bandido* photos. They welcome guests to sing along to the music, both live and recorded. Call to confirm hours.

More Zihuatanejo choices (in declining order of volume) include **Black Bull** (corner of N. Bravo and V. Guerrero, tel. 755/554-2230), a younger-crowd disco; **Rick's** (on Cuauhtémoc downtown, tel. 755/554-2535), live music nightly, from around 6 P.M., sometimes shows, popular with sailboaters; the **Bay Club** (tel. 755/554-4844), on the clifftop road to Playa La Ropa, with panoramic bay view, live evening jazz; and the upscale **Coconuts Lounge-Bar** (on Guerrero, a block from the beach, tel. 755/554-2518) and restaurant, relaxing garden setting, with hammocks, sofas, and videos.

Several Ixtapa hotel lobbies bloom with dance music from around 7 P.M. during the high winter season. Year-round, however, good medium-volume groups sometimes play for dancing evenings at the **Presidente Intercontinental** (tel. 755/553-0018); the **Barceló** (tel. 755/555-2000); and the **Las Brisas** (tel. 755/553-2121). Programs change, so call ahead to confirm.

Christine (in the Hotel NH Krystal, tel. 755/553-0333, open 10 P.M. Wed.–Sat., cover $10 women, $20 men) is Ixtapa's big-league discotheque. Patrons warm up by listening to relatively low-volume rock, watch videos, and talk while they can still hear each other. That stops around 11:30 P.M., when the fogs descend, the lights begin flashing, and the speakers boom forth their 200-decibel equivalent of a fast freight train roaring at trackside. Call to verify times.

TOURIST SHOWS

Ixtapa hotels stage **Fiesta Mexicana** extravaganzas, which begin with a sumptuous buffet and go on to a whirling skirt-and-sombrero folkloric ballet. After that, the audience becomes part of the act, with piñatas, games, cockfights, and dancing, while enjoying drinks from an open bar. In the finale, fireworks often boom over the beach, painting the night sky in festoons of reds, blues, and greens.

Entrance runs about $40 per person, with kids under 12 usually half price. The most reliable and popular shows (often seasonally only, sometimes hotel guests only) are staged on Saturday at the **Presidente Intercontinental** (tel. 755/553-0018); Tuesday at the **Dorado Pacífico** (tel. 755/553-2025); and Wednesday at the **Barceló** (tel. 755/555-2000). Usually open to the public; call ahead for confirmation and reservations.

SUNSETS

Sunsets are tranquil and often magnificent from the **(Restaurant/Bar El Faro** (tel. 755/553-1027, 5:30–10 P.M. daily low season, longer hours high season), which even has a cableway (7 A.M.–7 P.M.) that you can ride uphill from the south end of the Ixtapa beach. Many visitors stay to enjoy dinner and the relaxing piano bar. Reservations are recommended during winter and on weekends. Drive or taxi via the uphill road toward the Hotel Las Brisas Ixtapa, east of the golf course; at the first fork, head right for El Faro.

For equally brilliant sunsets in a lively but refined setting, try the 🔲 **lobby bar of the Hotel Las Brisas Ixtapa** (tel. 755/553-2121). Happy hour runs 6–7 P.M.; piano bar or seasonal live music for dancing begins around 7:30 P.M. (call to confirm programs). Drive or taxi along the uphill road at the golf course, following the signs to the crest of the hill just south of the Ixtapa beach.

Zihatanejo Bay's west-side headland blocks most Zihuatanejo sunset views, except for spots at the far end of Playa La Ropa. Here, guests congregate at the longtime beachfront favorite **Restaurant La Perla** (tel. 755/554-2700, 10 A.M.–10 P.M. daily).

CRUISES

Those who want to experience a sunset party while at sea ride the big 75-foot catamaran *Picante,* which leaves from the Zihuatanejo pier (call to confirm schedule) around 5:00 P.M. daily, returning around 8 P.M. The tariff runs about $50 per person, including open bar.

The *Picante* also heads out daily on a Sunshine Cruise around 10 A.M., returning around 2:30 P.M. Included are open bar, lunch, and snorkeling, for about $80 per person. Book tickets (high-season reservations mandatory) for both of the above cruises, which customarily include transportation to and from your hotel, through a hotel travel agent or directly through the *Picante* office (tel. 755/554-2694 or 755/554-8270, picante@picantecruises.com, www.picantecruises .com) at Puerto Mío, the small marina about half a mile across the bay from town. Get there via the road that curves around the western, right-hand shore of Zihuatanejo Bay.

MOVIES

Head over to the petite **Cine Paraíso** (on Cuauhtémoc, tel. 755/554-2318), three blocks from the beach in downtown Zihuatanejo, to escape into American pop, romantic comedy, and adventure. About the same is available daily from 4:30 P.M. at **Cine Flamingos** (tel. 755/553-2490), in the rear of the La Puerta shopping plaza across the boulevard from the Hotel Presidente Intercontinental, behind the *supermercado.*

Sports and Recreation

SWIMMING AND SURFING

Oft-calm Zihuatanejo Bay is fine for swimming and sometimes good for boogie boarding and bodysurfing at Playa Madera. On Playa La Ropa, although waves generally break too near shore for either bodysurfing or boogie boarding, swimming beyond the breakers is fine. Surfing is very rewarding at Playa Las Gatas, where swells sweeping around the south-end point give good, rolling left-handed breaks.

Heading northwest to more open coast, waves improve for bodysurfing and boogie boarding along Ixtapa's main beach Playa del Palmar, while usually remaining calm and undertow-free enough for swimming beyond the breakers. As for surfing, good breaks

sometimes rise off the Playa Escolleros marina jetty at the west end of Playa del Palmar.

Along Ixtapa's outer beaches, swimming is great along oft-calm Playa Quieta; surfing, bodysurfing, and boogie boarding are correspondingly good but hazardous in the sometimes mountainous open-ocean surf of Playa Linda and Playa Larga farther north.

Surfing lessons have arrived in Zihuatanejo, at **Catcha L' Ola** (Catch a Wave, in Ixtapa in the Centro Comercial Kiosko, behind Mama Norma and Deborah restaurant, tel. 755/553-1384, catchalola333@prodigy .net.mx, www.ixtapasurf.com). Besides surfing lessons and luxury camping trips to the best local surfing beaches, Catcha L' Ola offers board and equipment rentals and repair, and for-sale accessories equipment, information, and cheap beer.

SNORKELING AND SCUBA DIVING

Clear offshore waters (sometimes up to 100-foot visibility during the dry winter–spring season) have drawn a steady flow of divers and nurtured professionally staffed and equipped dive shops. Just offshore, good snorkel and scuba spots, where swarms of multicolored fish graze and glide among the rocks and corals, are accessible from **Playa Las Gatas** in Zihuatanejo Bay and **Playa Carey** on Isla Grande.

Many boat operators take parties for offshore snorkeling excursions. On Playa La Ropa, contact the aquatics shop at the foot of the hill beneath Beach Resort Sotavento. Playa Las Gatas, easily accessible by boat for $4 from the Zihuatanejo pier, also has snorkel and excursion boat rentals. In Ixtapa, similar services are available at beachfront shops at many of the hotels, such as the Posada Real, the NH Krystal, and the Presidente Intercontinental.

Other even more spectacular offshore sites, such as Morros de Potosí, El Yunque, Bajo de Chato, Bajo de Torresillas, Piedra Soletaria, and Sacramento, are accessible with the help of professional guides and instructors.

A pair of local dive shops stands out. In Zihuatanejo, licensed long-time instructors Carlos Bustamante and L. Ricardo Gutiérrez carry on Zihuatanejo's professional scuba tradition with **Nautilus Divers** (Juan Álvarez 33, tel. 755/554-9191, local cell tel. 044-755/102-3738, nautilus@nautilus-divers.com, www.nautilus-divers.com), two blocks west of the Zihuatanejo beachfront plaza. They begin with the resort course, with two hours' pool instruction and a guided dive, for $80. At the expert end, open-water NAUI certification takes three or four days and runs about $450. For certified divers (bring your certificate) they offer night, shipwreck, deep-water, and marine biology dives at more than three dozen coastal sites.

© BRUCE WHIPPERMAN

Surfing is fine on the rollers that curl around the eastern point of Zihuatanejo Bay at Playa Las Gatas.

Carlo Scuba (Playa Las Gatas, tel. 755/554-6003, carloscuba@yahoo.com, www .carloscuba.com) also provides professional scuba services. The PADI-trained instructors offer a resort course, including one beach dive ($65); a five-day open-water certification course ($450); and a two-tank dive trip for certified participants ($85, one tank $65). They also conduct student referral courses and night dives. Contact the manager-owner, friendly Jean-Claude Duran (known locally as Jack Cousteau), and his son Thierry, at their shop in the middle of Playa Las Gatas.

FISHING

Surf or rock casting with bait or lures, depending on conditions, is generally successful in local waters. Have enough line to allow casting beyond the waves (about 50 feet out on Playa La Ropa, 100 feet on Playa del Palmar and Playa Linda).

The rocky ends of Playas La Ropa, La Madera, del Palmar, and Las Gatas on the mainland, and Playa Coral on Isla Grande, are also good for casting.

For deep-sea fishing, you can launch your own boat or rent one. *Pangas* (launches) are available for hire from individual fishermen on the beach, or the boat cooperative (see below) at Zihuatanejo pier, or aquatics shops of the Beach Resort Sotavento on Playa La Ropa or the Hotels Las Brisas Ixtapa, Barceló, NH Krystal, and others on the beach in Ixtapa. Rental for a seaworthy *panga*, including tackle and bait, should run about $100 per half day, depending upon the season and your bargaining skill. An experienced boatman can typically help you and your friends hook six or eight big fish in about four hours; local restaurants are often willing to serve them as a small banquet for you in return for your extra fish.

BIG-GAME SPORTFISHING

Zihuatanejo has long been a center for billfish (marlin, swordfish, and sailfish) hunting. Most local captains have organized themselves into cooperatives, which visitors can contact either directly or through town or hotel travel agents. Trips begin around 7 A.M. and return 2–3 P.M. Fishing success depends on seasonal conditions. If you're not sure of your prospects, go down to the Zihuatanejo pier around 2:30 P.M. and see what the boats are bringing in. During good times they often return with one or more big marlin or swordfish per boat (although captains are increasingly asking that billfish be set free after the battle has been won). Fierce fighters, the sinewy billfish do not make the best eating and are often discarded after the pictures are taken. On average, boats bring in two or three other large fish, such as *dorado* (dolphinfish or mahimahi), yellowfin tuna, and roosterfish, all more highly prized for the dinner table.

The biggest local sportfishing outfitter is the blue-and-white fleet of the **Sociedad Cooperativa Teniente Azueta** (tel./fax 755/554-2056, 6 A.M.–6 P.M. daily), named after the naval hero Lieutenant José Azueta. You can see many of its several dozen boats bobbing at anchor adjacent to the Zihuatanejo pier. Arrangements for fishing parties can be made through hotel travel desks or at the cooperative office at the foot of the pier. The largest 36-foot boats, with four or five lines, go out for a day's fishing for about $450. Twenty-five-foot boats with three lines run about $250 per day; smaller *pangas,* about $180.

The smaller (18-boat) **Sociedad Cooperativa Triangulo** (tel./fax 755/554-3758, 9 A.M.–7 P.M. daily) is trying harder. Its 36-foot boats for six start around $350; a 25-footer for four, about $180. Contact the office across from the naval compound, near the west end of Paseo del Pescador.

A couple blocks away from the Zihuatanejo pier, find **Whiskey Water World** (Armada de Mexico 27, tel./fax 755/554-0147, local cell tel. 044-755/102-3779, U.S. tel. 661/310-3298, whiskey@prodigy.net.mx, www.zihuatanejo sportfishing.com.mx, www.ixtapasportfishing .com), that claims to employ only sober captains. Its top-of-the-line-only boats run from 25 feet ($200) upwards to 40 feet ($350), including license, bait, and soft drinks. Jack

Daniel's is extra. Proud members of the IGFA (International Game Fishing Association) and the Billfish Foundation, their captains follow marlin, swordfish, sailfish, tuna, and *dorado* tag-and-release policy.

Note: Prices quoted by sportfishing providers often (but not necessarily) include fishing licenses, bait, tackle, and amenities such as beer, sodas, ice, and on-board toilets. Such details should be pinned down (ideally by inspecting the boat) before putting your money down.

SPORTFISHING TOURNAMENTS

Twice a year, usually in May and January, Zihuatanejo fisherfolk sponsor the **Torneo de Pez Vela** (Sailfish Tournament), with prizes for the biggest catches of sailfish, swordfish, marlin, and other varieties. The entrance fee runs around $800, and the prizes usually include a new pickup truck, outboard motors, and other goodies. For information, contact the local sportfishing cooperative, Sociedad Cooperativa Teniente José Azueta (Muelle Municipal, Zihuatanejo, Guerrero 40880, tel. 755/554-2056), or the fishing tournament coordinator, Crecencio Cortés (tel. 755/554-8423).

However, in recognition that mass killing of billfish and other favorite deepwater fish, such as tuna, dolphinfish (*dorado*), and roosterfish (*pez gallo*) cannot continue forever, many local fishing outfitters, in cooperation with the conservationist Billfish Foundation, have had success sponsoring an annual Ixtapa-Zihuatanejo **Fintastic Tag and Release Tournament** where fish are returned to the sea alive after being caught. For more information, contact Whiskey Water World (listed earlier), email info@fintastic.com, or visit www.fintastic .com/zih-tour.

SAILING, SAILBOARDING, AND SEA KAYAKING

The tranquil waters of Zihuatanejo Bay, Ixtapa's Playa del Palmar, and the quiet strait off Playa

Zihuatanejo's Playa La Ropa rates as one of the loveliest best-for-everything beaches on the Mexican Pacific coast.

Quieta are good for these low-power aquatic sports. Shops on Playa La Ropa (at Beach Resort Sotavento and Catalina) in Zihuatanejo Bay and at beachfront at Ixtapa hotels, such as the NH Krystal, Presidente Intercontinental, and Dorado Pacífico, rent small sailboats, sailboards, and kayaks by the hour.

LAGOON KAYAKING AND BIRDWATCHING

The grand Laguna de Potosí and the smaller, more remote Estero Valentin, respectively about 10 and 20 miles (16 and 32 km) southeast of Zihuatanejo, have become prime wildlife-viewing sites, due to the enterprise of Ixtapa-based **Zoe Kayak Tours** (contact Brian, tel. 755/553-0496, zoe5@aol.com, www.zoe kayaktours.com). The earnest, wildlife-sensitive operators conduct thoroughly professional excursions, designed to maximize the quality of participants wildlife-viewing experience and appreciation. Itineraries vary, from full-day (Potosi, $80; Valentin, $100) outings to extended overnights and more.

MARINA AND BOAT LAUNCHING

Marina Ixtapa (tel./fax 755/553-2180, 755/553-0222, or 755/553-2365, ezuniga@ marinaixtapa.com or info@marinaixtapa.com, www.marinaixtapa.com), at the north end of Paseo Ixtapa, offers excellent boat facilities. The slip charge runs about $1 per foot per day, for 1–6 days ($0.75 for 7–29 days), subject to a minimum charge per diem. This includes use of the boat ramp, showers, pump-out, electricity, trash collection, mailbox, phone, fax, and satellite TV. For reservations and information, contact the marina 9 A.M.–2 P.M. and 4–7 P.M. daily, at the harbormaster's office in the marina-front white building on the right a block before the big white lighthouse.

The smooth, gradual Marina Ixtapa **boat ramp,** open to the public for a ramp fee (from about $40), is on the right-hand side street, leading to the water, just past the big white lighthouse. Get your ticket beforehand from the harbormaster.

GOLF AND TENNIS

Ixtapa's 18-hole professionally designed **Campo de Golf** is open to the public. In addition to its manicured 6,898-yard course, patrons enjoy full facilities, including pool, restaurant, pro shop, lockers, and tennis courts. Golf greens fee runs about $65, cart $30, club rental $25, 18 holes with caddy $20. Play goes on 7 A.M.–5:30 P.M. daily. The clubhouse (tel. 755/553-1062) is off Paseo Ixtapa, across from the Hotel Barceló. Reservations are accepted; morning golfers, get in line early during the high winter season.

The **Marina Golf Course** (tel. 755/553-1410 or 755/553-1424) offers similar services (greens fee $55, cart $30, club rental $30, caddy $20).

Ixtapa has virtually all of the local **tennis** courts, all of them private. The Campo de Golf has some of the best. Rentals run about $7/hour days, $10 nights. Reservations (tel. 755/553-1062) may be seasonally necessary. A pro shop rents and sells equipment. A teaching professional offers lessons for about $25 per hour.

Some hotels welcome outside guests at their tennis courts. Call the **Dorado Pacífico** (tel. 755/553-2025) or the **Las Brisas** (tel. 755/553-2121) for a reservation.

HORSEBACK RIDING

"Spiderman" Margarito, manager of the stable at **Playa Linda,** rents horses daily for beach riding for about $15 per hour low season, $20 high. Travel agencies and hotels offer the same, although for higher prices.

BICYCLING

Ixtapa's newest popular pastime is bicycling along the new 10-mile (16-km) round-trip *ciclopista* bike path to Playa Linda. The rental station is on the main boulevard, Paseo Ixtapa, in front of the Hotel Park Royal, about two blocks north of the north end of the Ixtapa shopping and restaurant complex. Bargain for a discount on the steep $10/hour asking rate.

The *ciclopista* takes off north, at the Paseo Las Garzas intersection, at the west-end corner of the Ixtapa shopping-restaurant complex.

Officially the *ciclopista* ends five miles (8 km) west, at the wooden bridge and crocodile-viewing point at the Playa Linda parking lot, but you can go 1.5 miles (2.5 km) farther to Barrio Viejo village at the lagoon's edge. Be sure to take a hat, water, and insect repellent.

If, on your return approach to Ixtapa, you haven't enjoyed your fill of bicycling, you can rack up more mileage along the Zihuatanejo *ciclopista* leg: Heading back to Ixtapa, about 100 yards after the intersection that directs traffic left to Highway 200, bear left where Paseo de los Pelicanos forks left and follow the Zihuatanejo *ciclopista* past the back (northwest) side of the golf course, another eight miles (13 km), two hours (leisurely) to Zihuatanejo and return.

WALKING AND JOGGING

Zihuatanejo Bay is strollable from Playa Madera all the way west to Puerto Mío. A relaxing half-day adventure could begin by taxiing to the Hotel Irma (Av. Adelita, Playa Madera) for breakfast. Don your hats and follow the stairs down to Playa Madera and walk west toward town. At the end of the Playa Madera sand, head left along the *andador* (walkway) that twists along the rocks, around the bend toward town. Continue along the beachfront Paseo del Pescador; at the west end, cross the lagoon bridge, head left along the bayside road to **Puerto Mío** resort and marina for a drink at the hotel's La Cala restaurant and perhaps a dip in the pool. Allow three hours, including breakfast, for this two-mile (3-km) walk; do the reverse trip during late afternoon for sunset drinks or dinner at the Irma.

Playa del Palmar, Ixtapa's main beach, is good for similar strolls. Start in the morning (during high winter–spring season) with breakfast (which is not served low season) at the Restaurant/Bar El Faro (tel. 755/555-2510 or 755/553-1027) atop the hill at the south end of the beach; open for breakfast high-season, 6 A.M.–noon daily. Ride the cableway or walk downhill. With the sun at your back stroll the beach, stopping for refreshments at the hotel pool patios en route. The entire beach stretches about three miles (5 km) to the marina jetty, where you can often watch surfers challenging

the waves and where taxis and buses return along Paseo Ixtapa. Allow about four hours, including breakfast.

The **reverse walk** would be equally enjoyable during the afternoon. Time yourself to arrive at the El Faro cableway about half an hour before sundown (7:30 P.M. summers, 5:30 P.M. winters) to enjoy the sunset over drinks and/or dinner. Get to El Faro by driving or taxiing via Paseo de la Roca, which heads uphill off the Zihuatanejo road at the golf course. Follow the first right fork to El Faro.

Adventurers who enjoy ducking through underbrush and scrambling over rocks might want to explore the acacia forest and wave-tossed rocky shoreline of the uninhabited west

ZIHUATANEJO, "PLACE OF WOMEN"

An oft-told Costa Grande story says that when Captain Juan Álvarez Chico was exploring at Zihuatanejo in 1522, he looked down on the round tranquil little bay lined with flocks of seabirds and women washing clothes in a freshwater spring. His Aztec guide told him that this place was called Cihuatlán, the "Place of Women." When Chico described the little bay, Cortés tacked "nejo" (little) on the name, giving birth to "Zihuatlanejo," which later got shortened to the present Zihuatanejo.

Investigators have offered a pair of intriguing alternative explanations for the "Place of Women" name, a handle that evokes visions of a land of Amazons. They speculate that either Isla Ixtapa (now Isla Grande) or the former royal bathing resort at Playa Las Gatas may have given rise to the name. The bathing resort, founded around 1400 by the Purépecha emperor, was most probably a carefully guarded preserve of the emperor's dozens of wives and female relatives. If not that, Isla Ixtapa may have been used as a refuge for the isolation and protection of women and children against the Aztec invaders who thus attached the label "Place of Women" to the locality.

side of **Isla Grande.** Take water, lunch, and a good pair of walking shoes.

Joggers often practice their art either on the smooth, firm sands of Ixtapa's main beachfront or on Paseo Ixtapa's sidewalks. Avoid crowds and midday heat by jogging early mornings or late afternoons. For even better beach jogging, try the flat, firm sands of uncrowded Playa Quieta about three miles (5 km) by car or taxi northwest of Ixtapa. Additionally, mile-long Playa La Ropa can be enjoyed by early-morning and late-afternoon joggers.

SPORTS EQUIPMENT
Deportes Náuticos (corner of N. Bravo and Guerrero, downtown Zihuatanejo, tel. 755/554-4411, 10 A.M.–2 P.M. and 4–9 P.M. Mon.–Sat.) sells snorkel equipment, boogie boards, tennis racquets, balls, and a load of other general sporting goods.

A pair of shops on Álvarez, near the pier, sell fishing equipment and supplies. Check out **Pesca Deportiva** (Álvarez 66, corner of Armada de Mexico, tel. 755/554-3651, 9 A.M.–2 P.M. and 4–7 P.M. Mon.–Sat.), which specializes in sportfishing rods, reels, lines, weights, and lures.

Alternatively, another shop a block east and across the street, **Articulos de Pesca** (Álvarez 35, tel. 755/554-6451, 9 A.M.–2 P.M. and 4–8 P.M. Mon.–Sat.) offers a similar selection of heavy-duty fishing goods.

Shopping

ZIHUATANEJO MARKET AND SHOPS
Every day is market day at the Zihuatanejo **mercado** on Avenida Benito Juárez, four blocks from the beach. Behind the piles of leafy greens, round yellow papayas, and huge gaping sea bass, don't miss the sugar and spice stalls. There you will find big cones of raw *panela* (brown sugar); thick, homemade golden honey; mounds of fragrant *jamaica* petals; crimson dried *chiles;* and forest-gathered roots, barks, and grasses sold in the same pungent natural forms as they have been for centuries.

For a huge, handy selection of everything, go to the big Kmart-style **Comercial Mexicana** (tel. 755/554-8321 or 755/554-8384, 8 A.M.–11 P.M. daily), behind the bus terminals on Highway 200, about a mile east (Acapulco direction) of downtown. Its shelves are stacked with a plethora of quality goods, from bread and bananas to flashlights and film.

For convenience shopping downtown by the beach, go to the small grocery **Adriana y Pancho,** at the plaza-front corner of Álvarez and Cuauhtémoc.

Handicrafts
Although stores in the Ixtapa Centro Comercial shopping center (described later) and the adjacent tourist market sell many handicrafts, Zihuatanejo shops offer the best overall selection and prices.

Sometime along your Zihuatanejo tour, be sure to visit the Zihuatanejo **Artisan Tourist Market** stalls, filled with a flood of attractive handicrafts brought by families who come from all parts of Mexico. Their goods—delicate Michoacán lacquerware, bright Tonalá papier-mâché birds, gleaming Taxco silver, whimsical Guerrero masks, rich Guadalajara leather—spread for blocks along Avenida Cinco de Mayo on the downtown west side. Compare prices; although bargaining here is customary, the glut of merchandise makes it a one-sided buyer's market, with many sellers barely managing to scrape by. If you err in your bargaining, kindly do it on the generous side.

Along the Paseo del Pescador
Private downtown Zihuatanejo shops offer an abundance of fine handicrafts. The best place

to start is on the beachfront Paseo del Pescador, at the **Casa Marina** shopping complex (tel. 755/554-2373, 10 A.M.–2 P.M. and 4–8 P.M. Mon.–Sat., credit cards generally accepted), a family project started by late community leader Helen Krebs Posse. Her adult children and their spouses own and manage stores on the bottom floor of the two-story building, just west of the beachfront town plaza.

The original store, **Embarcadero** (tel. 755/554-2373), on the lower floor, Avenida Álvarez side, has an unusually choice collection of woven and embroidered finery, mostly from Oaxaca. In addition to walls and racks of colorful, museum-quality traditional blankets, flower-embroidered dresses, and elaborate crocheted *huipiles,* they also offer wooden folk figurines and a collection of intriguing masks.

Other stores in the Casa Marina that you should visit include **La Zapoteca,** specializing in weavings from Teotitlán del Valle in Oaxaca. Also very worthwhile are **Metzli,** featuring all-Mexico crafts and resort wear selection, **El Jumil** (lacquerware and masks), and

Costa Libre (one-of-a-kind crafts and hammocks). Furthermore, Zapotec indigenous weavers from Oaxaca demonstrate their craft, often in the Embarcadero and La Zapoteca stores, mornings and afternoons November through April.

A block farther west on the Paseo del Pescador, find the **Mercado de Conchas** (Shell Market). Peruse the several stalls, with many fetching, priced-to-sell offerings including lovely seashells and shell jewelry, paintings, pottery, and much more.

Two blocks farther west, past the Sirena Gorda café, be sure to visit **Marea** clothing shop (8 A.M.–10 P.M. daily), across from the naval compound. It would be easy to pass, because of its mounds of ho-hum T-shirts out front, but if you look inside, you'll find racks stuffed with precious hand-crocheted *huipiles* and blouses from backcountry Guerrero and Oaxaca.

Along Avenida Cinco de Mayo

Return east two blocks along Avenida Álvarez and turn left, inland, at the corner of Cinco

© BRUCE WHIPPERMAN

Shell necklaces make attractive gifts to take back home.

de Mayo and find **Artesanías Olinalá** (Cinco de Mayo 2, tel. 755/554-9597, 9 A.M.–9 P.M. daily). Inside, you can enjoy a virtual museum of the venerable Guerrero lacquerware tradition, showcased by their seemingly endless collection of glossy boxes, trays, gourds, plates, and masks, all painstakingly crafted by age-old methods in the remote upcountry town of Olinalá. (After exiting Artesanías Olinalá you could conveniently visit the **Artisan Tourist Market** stalls on the other side of Cinco de Mayo.)

Continue up Cinco de Mayo, past the church, to **Art Nopal** (tel./fax 755/554-7530, 9 A.M.–9 P.M. daily in high season, opens 10:30 A.M. low season), the joy of the owner, who likes things from Oaxaca, especially baskets. He fills his shop with an organized clutter, including unique woven goods and ceramics.

Along Avenida Cuauhtémoc and More

Next, head right (east) one block along Bravo, to Cuauhtémoc, for a look through several more interesting shops.

At the corner, turn left, and continue a block, passing Ejido. A few doors farther, on the right, step into **Rosimar** (tel. 755/554-2864, 9 A.M.–9 P.M. daily), the creation of Josefina and Manuel Martínez. Inside, they offer a large priced-to-sell collection of Tonalá and Tlaquepaque pottery, papier-mâché, glassware, and more.

Head back down Cuauhtémoc. Turn left at Bravo, continuing another block, past Galeana, to **Galería Maya** (tel. 755/554-4606, 10 A.M.–2 P.M. and 5–9 P.M. Mon.–Sat.) in mid-block, on the left. Here, owner Tania Scales displays a multitude of one-of-a-kind folk curios from many parts of Mexico. Her wide-ranging, carefully selected collection includes masks, necklaces, sculptures, purses, blouses, *huipiles*, ritual objects, and much more. Furthermore, be sure not to miss Tania's favorites: several regal sculptures that represent a number of indigenous female deities, such as Ixta Bay, Maya jungle goddess; Coyolxauhqui, Aztec moon goddess; and Cihuateteo, representing all the women of Zihuatanejo.

Return to Cuauhtémoc, to **Alberto's** pair of shops (tel. 755/554-2161, 9 A.M.–9 P.M. daily, credit cards accepted), a few doors below the corner of Bravo, on opposite sides of the street. They offer an extensive silver jewelry collection. As with gold and precious stones, silver prices can be reckoned approximately by weight, at between $1 and $1.25 per gram. The cases and cabinets of shiny earrings, chains, bracelets, rings, and much more are products of a family of artists, taught by master craftsman Alberto, formerly of Puerto Vallarta, now deceased. Many of the designs are original, and, with bargaining, reasonably priced.

Continue another block downhill, past the corner of Ascencio, to **El Arte y Tradición** (tel. 755/554-4625, 10 A.M.–2 P.M. and 4–8 P.M. daily, credit cards accepted), where you can admire a lovely Talavera stoneware collection. This prized ceramic style, the finest of which is made by a few families in Puebla, comes in many shapes, from plates and vases to pitchers and tea cups. Talavera's colorful floral motifs originate from a fusion of traditions, notably Moorish, Italian, Turkish, and Persian, from the Mediterranean basin.

Now that you're again near the beachfront, for a treat head east along Avenida Álvarez, half a block past the plaza to **Cerámicas Tonalá** (Av. Álvarez 12B, tel. 755/554-6733, beach side, 9 A.M.–2 P.M. and 4–8 P.M. Mon.–Sat., credit cards accepted). Here you can view one of the finest Tonalá ceramics collections outside of the renowned source itself. Kindly owner Eduardo López's graceful glazed vases and plates, decorated in traditional plant and animal designs, fill the cabinets, while a menagerie of lovable owls, ducks, fish, armadillos, and frogs, all seemingly poised to spring to life, crowd the shelves.

IXTAPA SHOPS

Ixtapa's **Centro Comercial** complex stretches along the midsection of Paseo Ixtapa across from the hotels. Developers built about ten sub-complexes within the Centro Comercial, but several of them remain virtually empty. The good news is that the increasing stream of visitors to Ixtapa is adding new life to the Centro Comercial. At this writing, about six subcomplexes, most fronting the boulevard, are welcoming customers.

Los Patios, Las Fuentes, El Kiosco, and Las Palmas

Moving from south to north, first come the **Los Patios** and **Las Fuentes** subcomplexes, where designer stores occupy the choice boulevard frontages. Behind them, many small handicrafts stores and ordinary crafts and jewelry shops wait for customers along back lanes and inside patios.

Some stores stand out, however. Especially worth a look is the **La Fuente** (The Source, tel. 755/553-0812, 9 A.M.–9 P.M. daily), on the ground floor at the northeast corner of the Los Patios complex. The expertly selected all-Mexico handicrafts collection includes a treasury of picture frames, ranging from polished hardwood to mother-of-pearl; droll Day of the Dead figurines; lots of tinkling glass and ceramic bells; and a trove of women's blouses, dresses, and skirts, both traditional and stylishly up-to-date.

Also in Los Patios, you'll find at least three good Taxco silver shops and a gem of an embroidery store, **Artesanias Deshilados** (tel. 755/553-0221), with lovely tablecloths, curtains, *huipiles,* and much more.

At the **La Puerta** complex 100 yards farther on, a sprinkling of good restaurants and a cinema are open for business. There's also a **supermercado** (tel. 755/553-1514, 755/553-1508, 8 A.M.–11 P.M. daily) well stocked with veggies, fruit, groceries, and wine. An ATM, pharmacy, telecom money orders and fax are also available.

Behind the Los Patios, find the up-and-coming **El Kiosko** subcomplex, with a number of good restaurants and a surfing shop.

Next comes the boulevard-front **police station,** and, after that, the **Las Palmas** subcomplex (Señor Frog's, pharmacy, restaurant, Internet connection) and finally, the busy **Las Galerías** (mini-super, photo store, restaurant), at the corner of Paseo de las Garzas.

Information and Services

TOURIST INFORMATION

The local **Convention and Visitors Bureau** (Oficina de Convenciones y Visitantes, OCV, tel. 755/553-1270 or 755/553-1540, fax 755/553-0819, info@visit-ixtapa-zihuatanejo.org, www.vistit-ixtapa-zihuatanejo.org, 9 A.M.–2 P.M. and 5:30–8 P.M. Mon.–Sat.) information office is in Ixtapa near the south end of Avenida Gaviotas, the street that runs behind the Ixtapa Centro Comercial shopping complex. Call ahead to confirm hours. The generally helpful and knowledgeable staff answers questions, dispenses literature and maps, and can recommend tour agencies and guides.

PUBLICATIONS

The best local English-language book and magazine selection fills the many shelves of the **Hotel Las Brisas** shop (Paseo de la Roca, 9 A.M.–9 P.M. daily). Besides dozens of new paperback novels and scores of popular U.S. magazines, it stocks the *News* from Mexico City and *USA Today* and a small selection of Mexico coffee table books of cultural and historical interest.

In Zihuatanejo, the **newsstand** (8 A.M.–8 P.M. daily) across Juárez from the town market (near the corner of González) sells the *News.* A second newsstand, west end of the beachfront town plaza, in high season, stocks the *News* and some popular U.S. newspapers and magazines.

The small Zihuatanejo **Biblioteca** (public library, on Cuauhtémoc, 9 A.M.–8 P.M. Mon.–Fri., 9 A.M.–5 P.M. Sat.), five blocks from the beach, also has some shelves of English-language paperbacks.

TRAVEL AGENCIES AND TOUR GUIDES

A number of reliable local agents arrange and/or guide local excursions. One of the most experienced all-around is **Turismo International del Pacifico** (at Plaza Ixpamar in Ixtapa, tel. 755/554-2716 or 755/554-1173, tipzihua@prodigy.net.mx, www.ixtapa-zihuatanejo.net/tip, 9 A.M.–6 P.M. Mon.–Sat.). They offer air and hotel reservations, transportation, sportfishing, and many tours, from horseback riding and a one-day Acapulco tour, to a Playa Las Gatas beach party, and an all-day excursion to the cool, pine-tufted Michoacán highlands.

Eco-adventuring, including bicycling, kayaking, and snorkeling, is the specialty of **Adventours** (tel. 755/553-1069 or 755/553-1946, pablomendizabal@gmail.com, www.ixtapa-adventours.com).

Get way off the beaten track with very professional and wildlife-sensitive **Zoe Kayak Tours** (in Ixtapa, tel. 755/553-0496, zoe5@aol.com, www.zoekayaktours.com), which specializes in lagoon kayaking and birdwatching. For more information contact manager-guide Brian.

ECOLOGICAL ASSOCIATION AND HUMANE SOCIETY

The grassroots organization **SOS BAHIA** (Paseo del Pescador 9, info@sosbahia.org, www.sosbahia.org) sponsors efforts for local beach and lagoon cleanup and tree planting, to save the turtles, to stop the cruise-liner dock, and other projects. Their headquarters shares space with the Animal Protection Society on the upper floor of Casa Marina, just west of the Zihuatanejo beachfront plaza.

The family members of the late Helen Krebs Posse are the guiding lights of the **Sociedad Protectora de Animales** (Animal Protection Society, Paseo del Pescador 9, tel. 755/554-2373, cell tel. 044-755/112-1648, spaz@zihuatanejo.net, www.zihuatanejo.net/spaz/), which is working hard to educate people about animal issues. Contact one of the family members at the family's shop complex, in Casa Marina, just west of the Zihuatanejo plaza.

PHOTOGRAPHY

In Zihuatanejo, **Foto 30** (on Ejido, tel. 755/554-7610, 9 A.M.–8 P.M. Mon.–Sat., 10 A.M.–2 P.M. Sun.), between Galeana and Guerrero two blocks from the plaza, offers 30-minute process-and-print service and stocks lots of film and digital accessories, such as many cameras, including SLRs, and filters, tripods, and flashes.

In Ixtapa, **Foto Quick** (Paseo Ixtapa, tel. 755/553-1956, 9 A.M.–9 daily) offers approximately the same services and a modest selection of cameras and supplies, across the boulevard from Hotel Emporio.

MONEY EXCHANGE

Several banks, all with ATMs, cluster on the east side of downtown. Find **Banamex** (tel. 755/554-7293 or 755/554-7294), at the corner of Guerrero and Ejido two blocks from the beach, open for money exchange 9 A.M.–4 P.M. Monday–Friday and 10 A.M.–2 P.M. Saturday. If the Banamex lines are too long, use the ATM or walk to **Bancomer** (corner of Bravo and Juárez, tel. 755/554-7492 or 755/554-7493, 8:30 A.M.–4 P.M. Mon.–Fri., 10 A.M.–3 P.M. Sat.); or **Banco Santander Serfín** (tel. 755/554-3941, 9 A.M.–4 P.M. Mon.–Fri., 10 A.M.–2 P.M. Sat.) across the street.

After bank hours, go to either long-hours HSBC in Ixtapa (below) or to the center of town to **Casa de Cambio Guibal** (at Galeana and Ascencio, tel. 755/554-3522, fax 755/554-2800, 8 A.M.–8 P.M. daily), with long-distance telephone and fax two blocks from the beach, to change U.S., Canadian, French, German, Swiss, and other currencies and travelers checks. For the convenience, it offers you a few percent less for your money than the banks.

In Ixtapa, for long money-changing hours, go to **HSBC** (tel. 755/553-0642 or 755/553-0646, 8 A.M.–7 P.M. Mon.–Fri., 8 A.M.–3 P.M. Sat.) in front of the Hotel Emporio right on Paseo Ixtapa. Alternatively, go to **Bancomer** (tel. 755/553-2112 or 755/553-0525, 8:30 A.M.–4 P.M. Mon.–Fri.) in the Los Portales complex behind the shops across the boulevard from the Hotel Presidente Intercontinental.

COMMUNICATIONS

The single *correo* (post office, tel. 755/554-2192, 8 A.M.–6 P.M. Mon.–Fri., 9 A.M.–1 P.M. Sat.) that serves both Zihuatanejo and Ixtapa is in Zihuatanejo at Centro Federal, in the northeast corner of downtown, five blocks from the beach and about three blocks east of the Ixtapa minibus stop at Juárez and Morelos. Also in the post office is a sub-office of the very reliable government **Mexpost** (like U.S. Express Mail—upgraded, secure mail service).

Next door is **Telecomunicaciones**, which offers long-distance telephone, public fax (755/554-2163), telegrams, and money orders 8 A.M.–7 P.M. Monday–Friday. Another similar telecommunications office serves Ixtapa, in the La Puerta shopping center (rear side), across Paseo Ixtapa from the Hotel Presidente Intercontinental.

Money changer Casa de Cambio Guibal is also Zihuatanejo's private *larga distancia* telephone and fax office (on Galeana, corner of Bravo, tel./fax 755/554-3522, 8 A.M.–8 P.M. daily).

In both Ixtapa and Zihuatanejo, many **streetside public phone booths** provide relatively economical national and international (call the United States for about $1 per three minutes) long-distance service, using a Ladatel telephone card. Cards are readily available in grocery, drug, and liquor stores everywhere. First dial 001 for calls to the United States and Canada, and 01 for Mexico long-distance.

Beware of prominent "call home collect, dial 090" phone booths. Such calls customarily run about $30 per three minutes (whether or not you use the full three minutes.) Best ask the price before placing your call.

Get on the **Internet** in Zihuatanejo at one of several downtown spots, such as **Podernet** (on Ejido, 9 A.M.–10 P.M. daily), three blocks from the beach, between Cuauhtémoc and Cinco de Mayo.

In Ixtapa, answer your email at **Internet Connection Ixtapa** (tel. 755/553-2253, 8 A.M.–11 P.M. daily), in the Las Palmas subcomplex, behind Señor Frog's.

HEALTH AND EMERGENCIES

For medical consultations in English, contact U.S.-trained **IAMAT associate Dr. Rogelio Grayeb** (Bravo 71A, beach side, between Guerrero and Galeana, Zihuatanejo, tel. 755/554-3334, 755/553-1711, or 755/554-2040, fax 755/554-5041).

Another Zihuatanejo medical option is the very professional **Clínica Maciel** (Palmas 12, tel. 755/554-2380), which has a dentist, pediatrician, gynecologist, and surgeon on 24-hour call, two blocks east, one block north of the market.

Neither Ixtapa nor Zihuatanejo has any state-of-the art private hospitals. However, many local people recommend the state of Guerrero *hospital general* (on Av. Morelos, corner of Mar Egeo, just off from Hwy. 200, tel. 755/554-3965, 755/554-3650) for its generally competent, dedicated, and professional staff.

For medicines and drugs in Zihuatanejo, go to one of the several downtown pharmacies, such as **Farmacia La Principal** (Cuauhtémoc, two blocks from the beach, tel. 755/554-4217, 9 A.M.–9 P.M. Mon.–Sat.). In Ixtapa, go to **Farmapronto** pharmacy (with delivery service, tel. 755/553-2423, 8 A.M.–11 P.M. daily), in the Las Palmas subcomplex across the parking lot, north, from Señor Frog's.

For police emergencies in Ixtapa and Zihuatanejo, contact the *cabercera de policía* headquarters (on Calle Limón, Zihuatanejo, near Hwy. 200, tel. 755/554-2040). Usually more accessible are the police officers at the *caseta de policía* 24-hour police booth at the Zihuatanejo plaza-front, and in Ixtapa on Paseo Ixtapa, across from the Hotel Presidente Intercontinental. On Playa La Ropa, go to the small police station on the Paseo Costera, at the north-end intersection by the Hotel Villa del Sol.

IMMIGRATION

If you lose your tourist permit, go to **Migración** (on Colegio Militar, tel. 755/554-2795, 9 A.M.–1 P.M. Mon.–Fri.), about five blocks northeast of Plaza Kyoto, on the northeast edge of downtown. Bring your passport and some proof of the date you arrived in Mexico, such as your airline ticket, stamped passport, or a copy of your lost tourist permit. Although it's not wise to let such a matter go until the last day, you may be able to accomplish the needed paperwork at the airport Migración office (tel. 755/554-8480, 8 A.M.–9 P.M. daily). Call first.

LAUNDRY AND DRY CLEANING

In Zihuatanejo, take your laundry to **Lavandería Express** (on Cuauhtémoc, tel. 755/554-4393, 8 A.M.–8 P.M. daily), near the corner of González, five blocks from the beach.

If you also need something dry-cleaned, take it across the street to **Lavandería Premium** (8:30 A.M.–8 P.M. daily).

Getting There and Away

BY AIR

Nine reliable carriers connect Ixtapa-Zihuatanejo directly with U.S. and Mexican destinations year-round. A few more operate during the winter-spring high season.

Many **Aeroméxico** (reservations tel. 755/554-2018, flight information tel. 755/554-2237 or 755/554-2634) flights (and those of affiliate airline Aeroconnect) connect daily with Mexico City, where connections with U.S. destinations may be made.

Mexicana affiliate **Click Airlines** (reservations tel. 755/554-2208 or 755/554-2209, flight information tel. 755/554-2227) flights connect directly with Mexico City.

Alaska Airlines (direct from Mexico tel. 001-800/426-0333) connects directly with Los Angeles and San Francisco. For flight information and reservations.

US Airways (direction from Mexico 001-800/235-9292) connects with Phoenix.

Continental Airlines (tel. 755/554-2549, toll-free Mex. tel. 1-800/900-5000) connects with Houston daily.

Furthermore, a number of newcomers now connect Zihuatanejo with U.S. and Mexican destinations: **Frontier Airlines** (tel. 755/553-7025) with Denver; **Delta Airlines** (tel. 755/553-7146) with Los Angeles; **Interjet Airlines** (tel. 755/553-7002 or 755/553-7161) with Toluca; and **Alma Airlines** (toll-free Mex. tel. 01-800/800-2562, www.alma.com.mx) with Guadalajara.

A number of **seasonal and charter** flights operated by airlines such Air Canada, Frontier, Delta, American, and Northwest connect with northern U.S. and Canadian destinations during the winter. For more information, contact a travel agent or check the airlines' respective websites.

Air Arrival and Departure

Ixtapa and Zihuatanejo are quickly accessible, only about twenty minutes (seven miles/11 km) north of the airport via Highway 200. Arrival is generally simple—if you come with a day's worth of pesos (or an ATM card) and hotel reservations. Although the terminal does have an ATM (HSBC, in mid-terminal by the newsstand), a mailbox (*buzón*, outside the front opposite the check-in counters), restaurant, and shops for last-minute purchases, and newsstand with books, magazines, and *USA Today* (for $3.50), it has neither tourist information booth nor hotel-reservation service. Best arrive with a hotel reservation, and do not leave the choice up to your taxi driver, who will probably deposit you at a hotel that pays him a commission on your first night's lodging.

Transportation to town is usually by *taxi especial* (private taxi) or *colectivo* van. Tickets are available at booths near the terminal arrival exit. Tariff for a *colectivo* runs about $12 to both Ixtapa and Zihuatanejo, for a *taxi especial*, $28–37 for three or four people. Taxis to Troncones run about $75. Mobile budget travelers can walk the few hundred yards to the highway and flag down one of the frequent daytime Zihuatanejo-bound buses (very few, if any, continue to Ixtapa, however). At night, spend the money on a *colectivo* or taxi.

Several major **car rental** companies staff airport arrival booths. Avoid problems and save money by negotiating your car rental through the agencies' toll-free numbers before departure. Agents at the airport include **Hertz** (tel. 755/553-3338, 755/554-2255, or 755/554-2592, hertz_ixtapa@hotmail.com); **Budget** (tel. 755/554-4837 or 755/553-0397, ixtapa@budget ansa.com); **Alamo** (tel. 755/553-0206 or 755/554-8429, www.alamo-mexico.com.mx); **Thrifty** (tel. 755/553-7020 or 755/553-3019, aut zsa@prodigy.net.mx); **Dollar** (tel. 755/553-7050); and **Europcar** (tel./fax 755/553-7158 or 755/554-0869, www.europcar.com.mx).

Departure is quick and easy if you have your passport, tourist permit (which was stamped on arrival), and $19 cash (or the equivalent in pesos) international departure tax if your air ticket doesn't already cover it. Departees who've lost their tourist permits can avoid trouble and a fine by getting a duplicate from Zihuatanejo Immigration at the airport a few hours prior to departure. Simplify this procedure by being prepared with your passport and a copy of the lost permit or at least some proof of your date of arrival, such as an airline ticket.

BY CAR OR RV

Three routes, two easy and one formerly unsafe but now marginally recommended, connect Ixtapa-Zihuatanejo with Playa Azul and Michoacán to the northwest, Acapulco to the southeast, and Ciudad Altamirano and central Guerrero to the northeast.

Traffic sails smoothly along the 76 miles (122 km) of Highway 200, either way, between Zihuatanejo and Lázaro Cárdenas/Playa Azul. Allow about an hour and a half. Several miles before Lázaro Cárdenas the new Highway 37D *cuota* (toll) expressway allows easy access to highland central Michoacán (190 miles, 312 km, 4.5 hours to Uruapan, add another half-hour to Pátzcuaro) from Zihuatanejo. The same is true of the 150-mile (242-km, allow four hours) Highway 200 southern extension to Acapulco.

The story is different, however, for the winding, sparsely populated cross-Sierra Highway 134 (intersecting with Hwy. 200 nine miles/15 km north) from Zihuatanejo to Ciudad Altamirano. Rising along spectacular ridges, the paved but sometimes potholed road leads over cool, pine-clad heights and descends to the Ciudad Altamirano high, dry valley of the grand Río Balsas after about 100 miles (160 km). The continuing leg to Iguala on the Acapulco–Mexico City highway is longer, about 112 miles (161 km), equally winding and sometimes busy. Allow about eight hours westbound and nine hours eastbound for the entire trip. Keep filled with gasoline, and be prepared for emergencies, especially along the Altamirano–Zihuatanejo leg, where no hotels and few services exist. *Warning:* This route, unfortunately, was once plagued by robberies and nasty drug-related incidents. Before attempting this trip inquire locally—at your hotel, the tourist information office, or the bus station—to see if authorities deem the road safe.

BY BUS

Zihuatanejo has three major bus terminals. They stand side-by side on Highway 200, on the Acapulco-bound (east) side of town. The biggest and busiest is the big Estrella Blanca **Central de Autobús** station. Inside its shiny airline-style terminal, travelers have few services available: a battery of Ladatel card-operated telephones, a left-luggage service, and only a small snack bar. If you're going need supplies for a long bus trip, prepare by stocking up with water and food goodies before you depart.

Estrella Blanca (tel. 755/554-3477), the only carrier, computer-coordinates the service of its subsidiaries, including first-class Elite, Estrella Blanca, Futura, and luxury-class Turistar. Tickets are purchasable with either cash or credit cards for all departures from computer-assisted agents.

Many departures run along the Highway 200 corridor, connecting with Lázaro Cárdenas/ Playa Azul and northwestern destinations, such as Manzanillo, Puerto Vallarta, and the U.S. at Nogales and Tijuana, and with Acapulco and destinations southeast.

Several luxury- and first-class buses and some second-class buses connect daily with Acapulco. A number of them continue north to Mexico City, and at least one continues southeast along the Oaxaca coast all the way to Puerto Escondido and Salina Cruz. In the opposite direction, many luxury-, first-, and second-class buses (at least one an hour during the day) connect with Lázaro Cárdenas, Playa Azul junction, and northwest points.

Other departures connect north, via Michoacán. Among them, at least one daily departure connects north with points of Uruapan and Morelia, via the new 37D toll expressway. Another departure connects north by the expressway, via Uruapan, continuing northwest, via Guadalajara and Mazatlán all the way to the U.S. border at Mexicali and Tijuana.

Competing major bus carrier **Estrella de Oro** (tel. 755/554-2175) operates out of its separate station on the adjacent, west side of the Estrella Blanca station. It offers some long-distance first-class connections southeast along the coast via Acapulco, thence inland, via Chilpancingo, Iguala, and Taxco, to Mexico City.

Transportes Autobuses del Pacifico (TAP, tel. 755/554-2175), also operating out of the Estrella de Oro station, connects northwest, via Uruapan, Guadalajara, and Mazatlán, with Mexicali and Tijuana at the U.S. border.

A third major terminal, adjacent, west of the Estrella de Oro terminal, offers mostly first- and luxury-class departures, via a number of competent, well-equipped carriers, all of which can be reserved by calling 755/112-1002. They include **La Linea Plus**, with luxury-class departures connecting north with Guadalajara via Uruapan and also northwest with Puerto Vallarta, via Lázaro Cárdenas and Manzanillo; **Autovias,** with first-class departures connecting northeast with Mexico City, via Morelia and Toluca; **Parhikuni,** with first-class departures connecting northeast with Morelia, via Uruapan; **Omnibus de Mexico,** with first-class departures connecting north with Monterrey; and **Primera Plus,** with luxury-class departures connecting northeast, with Irapuato, Leon, and Aguascalientes.

South of Ixtapa and Zihuatanejo

Playa Las Pozas, Playa Blanca, and Barra de Potosí, the trio of pocket paradises not far southeast of Zihuatanejo and long known by local people, are now being discovered by a growing cadre of off-the-beaten-track seekers of heaven on earth. Taken together, they offer a feast of quiet south-seas delights: good fishing, beachcombing, camping, wildlife-viewing, and comfortable, reasonably priced lodgings.

Playa Las Pozas, a surf-fishing and seafood haven, is reachable via the Zihuatanejo airport road. A pair of palm-shaded bungalows offers comfortable accommodation. Playa Blanca, a mile farther southeast, is a long, lovely golden-sand beach, decorated by a lovely boutique hotel and restaurant. A few miles farther, Barra de Potosí village offers the ingredients of a heavenly one-day or one-week tropical excursion: palm-shaded seafood *palapas,* room for tent or RV camping, stores for supplies, a wildlife-rich mangrove lagoon, and a long beach, ripe for swimming, surfing, fishing, and beachcombing. A trio of petite bed-and-breakfast lodgings and a downscale beachfront hotel offer accommodation.

PLAYA LAS POZAS

Playa Las Pozas rewards visitors with a lagoon full of bait fish, space for RV or tent camping (be careful of soft sand), a wide beach, and friendly beachside *palapa* restaurants. The beach itself is 100 yards wide, of yellow-white sand, and extends for miles in both directions. It has driftwood but not many shells. Fish thrive in its thunderous, open-ocean waves. Consequently, casts from the beach can yield five-pound catches by either bait or lures. Local folks catch fish mostly by net, both in the surf

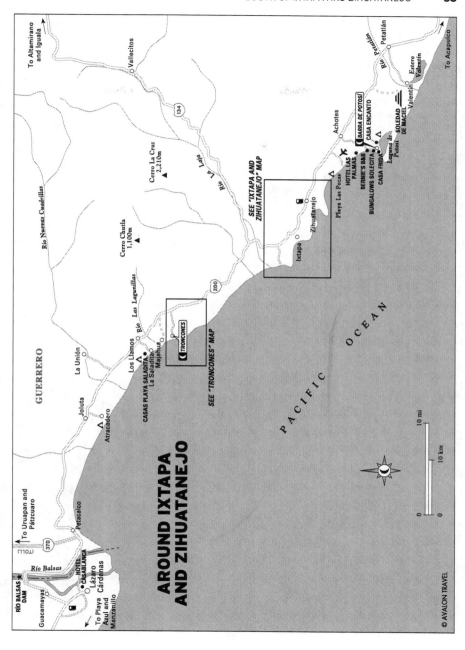

AROUND IXTAPA AND ZIHUATANEJO

© AVALON TRAVEL

and the nearby lagoon. During the June–September rainy season, the lagoon breaks through the bar. Big fish, gobbling prey at the outlet, can themselves be netted or hooked at the same spot.

Camping is popular here on weekends and holidays. Other times you may have the place to yourself. As a courtesy, ask at the friendly family-run *palapa* restaurant (on the west end by the lagoon) if it's okay to camp nearby.

Get to Playa Las Pozas by following the well-marked airport turnoff road at Km 230. After one mile, turn right before the cyclone wire fence just before entering the terminal complex and follow the bumpy but easily passable straight level road 1.1 miles (1.8 km) to the beach.

PLAYA BLANCA

In 2001, personable, savvy, and hardworking owner-builders from Phoenix, Arizona, decided to create heaven on lazy, lovely Playa Blanca. The result was ((**Hotel Las Palmas** (cell tel. 044-755/557-0634, from U.S. dial 011-52-1-755/557-0634, hotellaspalmas@ hotmail.com, www.hotellaspalmas.net), replete with precious architecture-as-art, including polished natural tree-trunk-beamed ceilings,

elegant tropical hardwood shutters, and massive overhanging thatched *palapa* roofs. A recipe for paradise? Yes, but there's even more: a big blue pool, a good restaurant and bar, all set in cool green grassy grounds overlooking a long, creamy, yellow-white strand. Their six super-comfortable handcrafted rooms, four with air-conditioning, two with ceiling fans, $225 d high season, $150 d low (June–Oct.) come with breakfast, but without TV or phones. No credit cards accepted nor kids under 18; not wheelchair accessible. Get there by continuing about 1.5 miles (2.5 km) along the beach road from Playa Las Pozas to Playa Blanca and Hotel Las Palmas. Reservations can be made through the hotel or the owners' Arizona agent, Gold Coast Travel (335 W. Virginia Ave., Phoenix, AZ 85003-1020, fax 602/253-3487, goldcoast-travel@hotmail.com).

((BARRA DE POTOSÍ

At Achotes, on Highway 200, nine miles (15 km) south of Zihuatanejo, a Laguna de Potosí sign points right to Barra de Potosí, an idyllic fishing hamlet at the sheltered south end of the Bahía de Potosí. After a few miles through green, tufted groves, the paved road parallels

Barra de Potosí offers both comfortable lodgings and tropical country ambience.

the bayside beach, a crescent of fine white sand, with a scattering of houses, a few comfortable bed-and-breakfasts, and one modest beachfront hotel.

The waves become even more tranquil at the beach's southeast end, where a sheltering headland rises beyond the village and the adjacent broad lagoon. Beneath its swaying palm grove, the hamlet of Barra de Potosí (pop. 1,000) has all the ingredients for tranquil living. Several broad, hammock-hung *palapa* restaurants (here called *enramadas*) front the bountiful lagoon.

Sights and Recreation

Home for flocks of birds and waterfowl and shoals of fish, the **Laguna de Potosí** stretches for miles to its far mangrove reaches. Adventure out with your own boat or kayak, or go with Orlando (ask at Restaurant Teresita), who regularly takes parties out for fishing or wildlife-viewing tours. Bring water, a hat, and insect repellent.

If you want to do more but don't have your own kayak, Ixtapa-based **Zoe Kayak Tours** (tel. 755/553-0496, zoe5@aol.com, www.zoekayaktours.com) leads kayaking trips on Laguna de Potosí's pristine waters.

Bait fish, caught locally with nets, abound in the lagoon. Fishing is fine for bigger catches (jack, snapper, mullet) by boat or casts beyond the waves. Launch your boat easily in the lagoon, then head past the open sandbar like the local fishermen.

Accommodations and Food

In the village, a pair of bed-and-breakfast-style hotels offer lodging. First consider the charming flower-bedecked **Casa del Encanto** (House of Enchantment, local cell 044-755/104-6709, from U.S. 011-52-1-755/104-6709, lauragecko2@hotmail.com, www.casadelencanto.com), on a village side street. Owner Laura Nolo rents her lovingly decorated rooms for $75–85 d low season, $90–115 d high (Oct. 31–May 1), including private hot-water bath and full breakfast; massage available at extra cost.

Beneath the plumy grove nearby, guests at **Casa Frida** (local cell 044-755/557-0049,

from the U.S. 011-52-1-755/557-0049, casa-frida@zihuatanejo.net, www.zihuatanejo.net/casafrida), life project of Mexican-French couple Anabella and François, enjoy fondly decorated rooms, built around a charmingly compact pool-patio garden. Room furnishings, based on a Frida Kahlo theme, include handcrafted art and furniture, mosquito curtains over the double beds, and bright Talavera-tiled hot-water bathrooms. François and Annabella enjoy hosting grand Christmas and Easter dinners; reserve ahead of time. Rates run about $90 d ($110 Christmas holiday), including breakfast; adults only, no pets, closed May 1–November 1.

On the beachfront, about half a mile from the village, settle into the lap of luxury at **Bungalows Solecito** (local cell 044-755/100-5976, from U.S 011-52-1-755/100-5976, www.bungalows-solecito.com, $115 s or d, $2500 mo.). Friendly owner-builder Manuel Romo offers 10 airy, rustic-chic south-seas bungalows for two, with kitchen, all artfully arranged around a flowery, palm-shadowed beachfront garden and pool-patio. Stroll out just a few steps and you're on the lovelier-than-life Playa Barra de Potosí. Get your reservations in early.

About a mile out of the village, back toward Zihuatanejo, the downscale **Hotel Barra de Potosí** (Petatlán tel. 755/554-8290 or 755/556-8434, Zihuatanejo tel. 755/554-3445, fax 755/554-7060, reservaciones@hotelbarradepotosi.com.mx, www.hotelbarradepotosi.com.mx) perches right on the beach. The surf is generally tranquil and safe for swimming near the hotel, although the waves, which do not roll but break rather quickly along long fronts, do not appear good for surfing. The hotel, once rough and neglected, has been renovated and is maintained at a rather plain but habitable condition and the pool has been returned to a brilliant blue. The owner says that the restaurant will be open during the high winter season, but will close during the low summer and fall. The beach, however, remains inviting and kid-friendly year-round. The 14 rooms, in rising order of price, start with hot and stuffy interior rooms for about $35 d; improving to exterior rooms with view of the parking lot for $45 d, then better rooms with private oceanview balcony for $55 d, and finally kitchenette suite for four, also with oceanview balcony, $80. All come with fans, but only room-temperature water and bare-bulb lighting; bring your own lampshade or booklight.

About a mile farther from town on the same luscious beachfront, near the spot where the road from Achotes arrives at the beach, **Bernie's Bed and Breakfast** (local cell 044-755/556-6333, from U.S. 011-52-1-755/556-6333, playacalli@ hotmail.com, www.berniesbedandbreakfast .com) offers three comfortable rooms with "no TV, or piped-in-music" (says friendly owner Bernie Wittstock) that open onto a lovely palm-shadowed beachfront pool and patio. Rentals run about $90 s or d year-round except for $110 December 15–January 7 and Easter holiday, with breakfast. If you give him a day's notice, Bernie will cook a light meal for you.

Camping is common by RV or tent along the uncrowded edge of the lagoon. Village stores can provide basic supplies. Prepared food is available at about a dozen permanent lagoon-side *palapa* restaurants. **Restaurant Teresita** is especially recommended.

Getting There and Away

By car, get to Barra de Potosí by following the signed turnoff road from Highway 200 at Km 225, nine miles (14 km) south of Zihuatanejo, just south of the Río Los Achotes bridge. Continue along the good, mostly paved road; pass the hotel at Mile 5 (Km 8) and continue to the village at Mile 5.5 (Km 8.9). Alternatively, get to Barra de Potosí by continuing east about three miles (5 km) along the beach road from Hotel Las Palmas at Playa Blanca.

By bus, follow the same route via a Petatlán-bound bus (Omnibus de Mexico, Estrella Blanca) either from one of the Zihuatanejo bus stations, or the local Petatlán bus from the station on Zihuatanejo Avenida Las Palmas, across from Bancrecer. In either case, ask the driver to let you off at the Barra de Potosí turn-off at Achotes and wait for the Barra de Potosí–bound covered pickup truck (about every about 30 minutes daytime).

North of Ixtapa and Zihuatanejo

Visitors to Troncones and Majahua (mah-HAH-wah) can enjoy a long, pristine, coral-studded beach as well as the natural delights of a small kingdom of forested wildlife-rich hinterland that stretches for miles above and behind the beach. While Troncones has acquired a modicum of modern travel amenities, including a number of restful bed-and-breakfast inns and gourmet restaurants, Majahua remains charmingly rustic.

⬛ TRONCONES

Troncones (pop. 1,000) has a little bit of everything: shady seafood *ramadas,* cozy seaside inns and houses for rent, a sprinkling of good restaurants, and room to park your RV or set up a tent by the beach. Most folks get there by bus or taxi, from Ixtapa or Zihuatanejo via the side road off of Highway 200 about 20 miles (32 km) north of Ixtapa.

But that's just the beginning. Troncones has acquired a growing colony of North Americans, some of whom operate small accommodations for lovers of peace, quiet, and the outdoors. Besides lazing in hammocks and sunning on the sand, guests at all Troncones lodgings share the same luscious shoreline. You can swim, surf, bodysurf, and boogie board the waves, jog along the sand, explore a limestone cave, and thrill to a treetop cable adventure in the adjacent jungle. Back by the shore, you can beachcomb to your heart's content while enjoying views of the wildlife trove—fish, whales (Dec.–Mar.), dolphins, turtles (Nov.–Jan.), swarms of herons, boobies, egrets, and cormorants—that abounds in the ocean and in nearby lagoons.

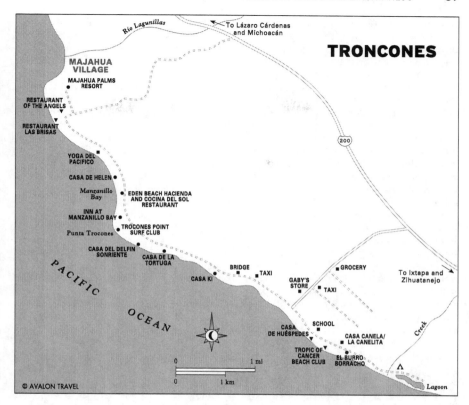

TRONCONES

Río Lagunillas

To Lázaro Cárdenas
and Michoacán

MAJAHUA
VILLAGE

MAJAHUA PALMS
RESORT

RESTAURANT
OF THE ANGELS

RESTAURANT
LAS BRISAS

200

YOGA DEL
PACIFICO

CASA DE HELEN

Manzanillo
Bay

EDEN BEACH HACIENDA
AND COCINA DEL SOL
RESTAURANT

INN AT
MANZANILLO BAY

TRONCONES POINT
SURF CLUB

Punta Troncones

CASA DEL DELFIN
SONRIENTE

CASA DE LA
TORTUGA

BRIDGE

TAXI

GROCERY

To Ixtapa and
Zihuatanejo

CASA KI

GABY'S
STORE

TAXI

PACIFIC

OCEAN

CASA
DE HUÉSPEDES

SCHOOL

CASA CANELA/
LA CANELITA

Creek

TROPIC OF
CANCER
BEACH CLUB

EL BURRO
BORRACHO

0   1 mi

0   1 km

© AVALON TRAVEL

Lagoon

Accommodations and Food

Many Troncones accommodations fall into
the $50–100 category. As you move north-
west (from the entrance road, turn right at the
beach) after the bridge, first comes 🄲 **Casa Ki**
(P.O. Box 405, Zihuatanejo, Guerrero 40880,
tel. 755/553-2815, casaki@yahoo.com, www
.casa-ki.com), the life project of Ed and Ellen
Weston, now managed by daughter Tina
Morse. Casa Ki (named for the Japanese
word for energy and wholeness) offers four immaculate, charmingly rustic cottages tucked in
a lovingly tended seaside garden compound.
Each cottage sleeps approximately two adults
and two children and comes with shower, toilet, fans, and refrigerator and daily maid service. Guests share a shady outside cooking and

dining *palapa*. High-season (Nov. 15–Apr. 30)
rentals run $95–115 d ($65–85 d low season)
for the cottages, including full breakfast high
season only. Tina also rents a lovely two-bedroom, two-bath house that sleeps up to six,
with full kitchen and daily maid service, for
about $220 high, $150 low (breakfast not included). Get your winter reservations in early.

After another quarter mile find **Casa de la
Tortuga** (P.O. Box 37, Zihuatanejo, Guerrero
40880, tel./fax 755/553-2812, casadelator-
tuga@yahoo.com or casadetortuga@troncones
.net), the original Troncones lodging, built
by friendly pioneer Dewey McMillin during
the late 1980s. Although he used to rent individual rooms, Dewey has lately been renting
the whole place (sleeping a dozen or more) for

about $350/day, $2,000/week, $7,500/month during the high season, with staff; guests supply their own food. Reservations are mandatory during the winter. Rates during the low May–October season are discounted about 20 percent. If business is too slow, Casa de la Tortuga closes June, July, and August.

Continuing another half mile, you'll find one of Troncones' longstanding gems, the **(Inn at Manzanillo Bay** (tel. 755/553-2884, fax 755/553-2883, manzanillobay@aol.com, www .manzanillobay.com, $105 d low, $128 high). Here, owner-chef Michael Bensal has realized his dream of paradise: a plumy haven of eight rustic-style *palapa*-roofed *cabañas,* comfortably furnished with deluxe amenities, set around a luscious blue swimming pool and leafy patio. Here you can have it all: a gently curving, wave-washed surfable shoreline, with the murmur of the billows at night and plenty of hammock time by day. There's a good restaurant and even TV if you want it, and breakfast is included. Send deposits for the full amount to P.O. Box 5306, Concord, CA 94524.

Finally, 100 yards farther along the beach, you arrive at the **Eden Beach Hacienda and La Cocina del Sol Restaurant** (P.O Box 128, Zihuatanejo, Guerrero 40880, tel. 755/553-2802, evaandjim@aol.com, www .edenmex.com, $105–140), which shares the same luscious tropical forest oceanfront as all the other lodgings. The amenities include 14 immaculate accommodations—six comfortable rooms with fan in the original house, four spacious beachfront suites with fan, and four beamed-ceiling, air-conditioned suites—all invitingly decorated in stucco and Talavera tile, with king-size beds and private hot-water bathrooms. Rates (Oct.–May) run $105 d in the main house, $120 on the beachfront, and $140 for the air-conditioning suites, all including breakfast. Make reservations with the hotel direct by phone or email. You may also write or fax them in the United States (41 Riverview Dr., Oak Ridge, TN 37830, fax 801/340-9883). Credit cards are not accepted.

At the opposite, southeast end of the Troncones beach, **(El Burro Borracho** (The

Troncones offers a number of restful bed-and-breakfast lodgings, such as the Inn at Manzanillo Bay.

© BRUCE WHIPPERMAN

Drunken Burro, P.O. Box 37, Zihuatanejo, Guerrero 40880, tel./fax 755/553-2834, tronconesburro@yahoo.com) beachfront *palapa* restaurant and inn has become a favorite stopping place for the growing cadre of daytime visitors venturing out from Ixtapa and Zihuatanejo. Here, owner Dewey McMillin continues the standard set by former owner-chef Michael Bensal with spicy shrimp tacos, rum-glazed ribs, jumbo shrimp grilled with coconut-curry sauce, and broiled pork chops with mashed potatoes. Besides the shady ocean-view *palapa* restaurant, El Burro Borracho offers six "elegantly simple" airy rooms, each with bath, in three stone duplex beachfront cottages. Rooms include king-size bed, rustic-chic decor, hot water, and fans. Shared cooking facilities are also available. Sports and activities include swimming, surfing, and boogie boarding, plus kayaks, for use of guests. Room rentals run about $65 d high season, $45 low, with continental breakfast.

For more choices, consider some of the platoon of newer guesthouses, bed-and-breakfast inns, hotels, and vacation rental villas that have recently sprouted on the Troncones beachfront. Many choices, mostly upscale, are available. They include a cluster of jointly managed houses—**Casa Alegria, Casa Canela, La Canelita,** and **Santa Benita**—with rentals varying from individual rooms to whole houses (P.O. Box 277, Zihuatanejo, Guerrero 40880, tel. 755/553-2800, casacanela@yahoo .com, www.tronconestropic.com/alegria, from $40 to $225); bed-and-breakfast **Casa del Delfin Sonriente** (Smiling Dolphin, tel. 755/553-2803, U.S. tel. 831/688-6578, enovey@sasq.net, $70 and up); deluxe-suite **Casa Colorida** (U.S. tel. 303/400-5442, fax 303/680-9685, annmerritt@aol.com, www .casacolorida.com, $200–280); and luxurious three-bedroom house **Casa de Helen** (tel. 755/553-2800, tronconeshelen@yahoo.com, www.tronconeshelen.com, $225–300). For information on more rentals, visit websites www .troncones.com.mx and www.zihuatanejo.net.

For camping or RV parking spots, turn south (left) at the beach and follow the road half a mile past several likely spots to pull off and camp. At the far southern end, a lagoon spreads beside a pristine coral-sand beach, which curls around a low hill toward a picture-perfect little bay. Stores back by the entrance road can supplement your food and water supplies. El Burro Borracho may also let you park your RV in their lot out front for a fee.

Sports and Recreation

Michael Bensal at the Inn at Manzanillo Bay arranges sealife-viewing tours and fully equipped launches for four hours of fishing for 2–4 people for about $150.

Surfing has become a major Troncones recreation. The most popular spot is the palm-tufted inlet, locally known as Manzanillo Bay, location of both the Inn at Manzanillo Bay and Eden Beach Hacienda. Lately, a pair of enterprising lovers of the tropics, Michael and Ann Linn of San Luis Obispo, California, operating as **ISA (Instructional Surf Adventures) Mexico** (cell tel. 044-755/558-3821, U.S. tel. 514/563-6944, surf@isamexico.com, www .isamexico.com), offer both local day instruction and extended surfing packages during the fall–winter (Nov.–Apr.) season. Classes are small and all equipment and deluxe beachfront lodging is customarily included in packages, which run about $1,000 per person, double occupancy.

Shopping and Services

Michael Bensal maintains a shop offering fine wines, Taxco silver, Cuban cigars, and surfboards new and used at his Inn at Manzanillo Bay. Eva Robbins, at Eden Beach Hacienda, also has both a gallery offering for-sale art and a shop, **Fruity Keiko,** with a charming collection mostly of Guerrero country crafts: baskets, toys, silver jewelry, silk scarves, and more.

The **Boutique** at the Tropic of Cancer Beach Club (from the Zihuatanejo entry road, turn left and continue about two blocks, to the Beach Club on the right) offers some decorative handicrafts, beachwear, a lending library, and some drugs and medications.

Folks interested in rentals or buying

property in Troncones should contact Dewey McMillin (tel. 755/553-2812, casadela tortuga@yahoo.com).

A few local stores provide drinking water and groceries. For example, on the Zihuatanejo entrance road, on the right as you enter the village, **Gaby's** (tel. 755/553-2891 or 755/553-2892) offers some produce, basic groceries, and a long-distance telephone.

Getting to Troncones

Follow the signed paved turnoff to Playa Troncones from Highway 200, around Km 30, about 18 miles (29 km) north of Zihuatanejo; or about 42 miles (73 km) south of the Río Balsas dam. Continue 2.2 miles (3.5 km) to the Playa Troncones beachfront *ramadas*. Turn left for the camping spots, the main part of the beach, and El Burro Borracho; turn right for the other described lodgings, beginning with Casa Ki, about a mile farther along the beachfront forest road. From there, the car-negotiable gravel road continues about 1.5 miles (2.5 km) along the beach to Playa Majahua.

MAJAHUA

Here you can enjoy a slice of this beautiful coast as it was before tourism bloomed at Troncones nearby. Instead of cell phones and the Internet, Majahua folks still enjoy plenty of palmy shade, stick-and-wattle houses, and lots of the fresh seafood served in about half a dozen hammock-equipped *ramadas* scattered along the beach. One of the *ramadas* is competently run by a friendly family who calls it **Restaurant de Los Angeles.** Another of the best choices is *palapa* **Restaurant Las Brisas,** next door.

Camping, moreover, is welcomed by local folks (although space, especially for RVs, is limited). Water is available, but campers should bring water or purifying tablets and food.

The beach curves from a rocky southeast point, past the lagoon of Río Lagunillas, and stretches miles northwest past shoreline palm and acacia forest. The sand is soft and dusky yellow, with mounds of driftwood and a seasonal scattering of shells. Waves break far out

and roll in gradually, with little undertow. Fine left-breaking surf rises off the southern point. Boats are easily launchable (several *pangas* lie along the beach) during normal good weather.

To get to Playa Majahua either along the beach road, northeast from Troncones, or directly, by following the signed turnoff from Highway 200 at Km 33, 20 miles (32 km) northwest of Zihuatanejo (just south of the Río Lagunillas bridge), or 44 miles (70 km) southeast of the Río Balsas dam. Continue 2.9 miles (4.7 km) to the beach.

BEYOND TRONCONES

This northwest corner of the Acapulco region hides a few small havens for those who yearn for their fill of fresh seafood, uncrowded beach camping, and plenty of swimming, surfing, fishing, and beachcombing. And finally, those who venture to Guerrero's extreme northwest edge can encounter the great Río Balsas, the Mexican Pacific's mightiest river, whose drainage basin extends over five states: Jalisco, Morelos, Michoacán, Guerrero, and Oaxaca.

La Saladita

At La Saladita (The Little Salty Lagoon), the day used to climax when the oyster divers would bring in their afternoon catches. Now, however, the oysters are all fished out. While the oysters recover, divers go for octopus and lobster which, broiled and served with fixings, sell for about $15 for a one-pounder. You can also do your own fishing via rentable (offer $20/hour) beach *pangas,* which go out daily and routinely return with three or four 20-pound fish.

The beach itself is level far out, with rolling waves fine for surfing, swimming, boogie boarding, and bodysurfing. There are enough driftwood and shells for a season of beachcombing. The beach spreads for hundreds of yards on both sides of the road's end. Permanent *palapa* restaurants **Paco, Ilianet,** and **Sotelo** supply shade, seafood, and camping space for about $5 per person. Camping is especially popular during the Christmas and

Easter holidays. Other times, you may have the whole place to yourself. Bring your own food and water; the small stores at the highway village may help add to your supplies.

Furthermore, a colony of comfortable lodgings has been built to serve the growing crowd of visitors who now frequent this formerly undiscovered mini-paradise. Moving up the economic scale, you can choose from a number of options: the rustic beachfront *cabañas,* offered by most of the *palapa* restaurants from about $20 d; or Sotelo restaurant's modest beachfront hotel, with about four plain rooms from about $35 d.

Alternatively, check out the **House of Waves** (tel. 755/554-4532, saladita@houseofwaves.net, www.houseofwaves.net), a two-story south-seas house on stilts, with comfortable rooms with two double beds, private baths, fans or air-conditioning, and a shared kitchenette, from about $65 for up to four; or, by Ilianet beachfront restaurant, **Casas Playa Saladita** (toll-free U.S. tel. 877/927-6928, info@casasplaya saladita.com, www.casasplayasaladita.com), eight very attractive and comfortable architect-built kitchenette apartments, with two double beds, hot-water baths and air-conditioning, about $80 lower level, upper level (better ocean view and breeze), $90.

To get to La Saladita, at Km 40, 25 miles (40 km) northwest of Zihuatanejo and 39 miles (63 km) southeast of the Río Balsas, turn off at the village of Los Llanos. After 0.2 mile, turn right at the church and continue another 3.1 miles (5.1 km) to the beach, where a left fork leads you to Sotelo *palapa* and a right fork leads to the "Embarcadero" sector of the beach and Paco's and Ilianet and other *palapa* restaurants.

Atracadero

A few miles farther northwest, Playa Atracadero is just being "discovered" and is less frequented than La Saladita. Its two or three beach *palapa* restaurants appear to operate only during weekends, holidays, and the fall–early winter surfing season. Crowds must gather sometimes, however: The main *palapa* has, over time, accumulated a five-foot pile of oyster shells.

The beach sand itself is soft and yellow-gray. The waves, with good, gradual surfing breaks, roll in from far out, arriving gently on the sand. Boat launching would be easy during calm weather. Little undertow menaces casual swimmers, bodysurfers, or boogie boarders. Lots of driftwood and shells—clams, limpets, snails—cover the sand. The beach extends for at least three miles (5 km) past palm groves on the northwest.

Furthermore, at the time of writing, workers are building a number of beachfront *cabañas* for rent, so by the time you arrive you'll probably have the company of a sprinkling of surfers and other fellow seekers of heaven on earth.

To get to Playa Atracadero, turn off at Highway 200 Km 64, near the hamlet of Joluta, 40 miles (64 km) northwest from Zihuatanejo and 24 miles (39 km) southeast from the Río Balsas. Bear left all the way, 2.1 miles (3.3 km) to the beach.

The Río Balsas

It's hard to remain unimpressed as you follow Highway 200 over the Río Balsas Dam for the first time. The dam marks the Michoacán–Guerrero state boundary. The hulking rock-fill barrier rises in giant stair-steps to its highway summit, where a grand lake mirrors the Sierra Madre, while on the opposite, downstream side, Mexico's greatest river spurts from the turbine exit gates 500 feet below. The river's power, converted into enough electric energy for a million Mexican families, courses up great looping transmission wires, while the spent river meanders toward the sea. To experience all this, drive directly over the dam, from either the north or south, by following old Highway 200 (bear inland) instead of taking the straight-line, toll expressway direct to or from Lázaro Cárdenas.

LÁZARO CÁRDENAS

The newish industrial port city of Lázaro Cárdenas, named for the Michoacán-born president famous for expropriating American oil companies, is an important transportation and service hub for the northwest Acapulco region. For travelers it's useful as a stopover

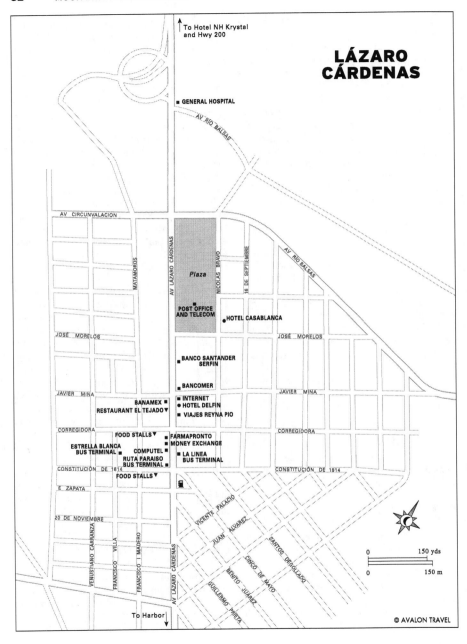

To Hotel NH Krystal and Hwy 200

LÁZARO CÁRDENAS

GENERAL HOSPITAL

AV. RIO BALSAS

AV. CIRCUNVALACION

MATAMOROS

AV LAZARO CARDENAS

NICOLAS BRAVO

16 DE SEPTIEMBRE

AV. RIO BALSAS

Plaza

POST OFFICE AND TELECOM

HOTEL CASABLANCA

JOSÉ MORELOS

JOSÉ MORELOS

BANCO SANTANDER SERFIN

BANCOMER

JAVIER MINA

JAVIER MINA

BANAMEX
RESTAURANT EL TEJADO▼

INTERNET
HOTEL DELFIN
VIAJES REYNA PIO

CORREGIDORA

CORREGIDORA

FOOD STALLS▼

FARMAPRONTO
MONEY EXCHANGE

ESTRELLA BLANCA
BUS TERMINAL

COMPUTEL

RUTA PARAISO
BUS TERMINAL

LA LINEA
BUS TERMINAL

CONSTITUCIÓN DE 1814

CONSTITUCIÓN DE 1814

FOOD STALLS▼

E. ZAPATA

20 DE NOVIEMBRE

VICENTE PALACIO

JUAN ALVAREZ

VENUSTIANO CARRANZA

FRANCISCO VILLA

FRANCISCO I MADERO

AV. LAZARO CARDENAS

SANTOS DEGOLLADO

CINCO DE MAYO

BENITO JUAREZ

GUILLERMO PRIETA

To Harbor

0   150 yds
0   150 m

© AVALON TRAVEL

mainly for services and bus connections, southeast with Ixtapa-Zihuatanejo, Acapulco, and Mexico City, northwest with the Michoacán coast, Manzanillo, and Puerto Vallarta, and north with the upland Michoacán destinations of Uruapan, Pátzcuaro, and Morelia. Most of its services, including banks, bus stations, post office, hospital, hotels, and restaurants, are clustered along north–south Avenida Lázaro Cárdenas, the main ingress boulevard, about three miles (5 km) from its Highway 200 intersection.

Accommodations and Food

If you decide to stay overnight, nearby hotels offer reasonably priced lodging. The most conveniently located is the **Hotel Delfín** (Av. L. Cárdenas 1633, tel. 753/532-1418), across the street from the Ruta Paraíso bus station. The approximately 20 rooms with baths, in three stories, cluster around an inner pool and patio. Rates run about $25 d, with fans, hot water, TV, and telephone; add air-conditioning for $35.

For more class, go to the high-rise (**Hotel Casablanca** (on Bravo, tel. 753/537-3480, 753/537-3481, 753/537-3482, 753/537-3483, or 753/537-3484, fax 753/532-4036), a block east from Avenida Lázaro Cárdenas, visible behind and above Bancomer. It offers about six floors of light and comfortable modern-standard deluxe rooms with panoramic private-balcony views. Downstairs, past the lobby, a restaurant overlooks an inviting rear pool and patio. Rooms cost $48 s, $76 d, with air-conditioning, phones, TV, and parking.

An even fancier hotel option is the executive-class **NH Krystal Express** (Av. Circuito de las Universidades 60, tel. 753/533-2900 or 753/533-2922, toll-free U.S. tel. 888/726-0528 or Can. tel. 866/299-7096, nhlazarocardenas@nh-hotels.com, www.nh-hotels.com) on the west side of the ingress boulevard Avenida Lázaro Cárdenas, at the traffic circle, about a quarter mile before the town center. It offers 120 deluxe rooms for about $150 d, with air-conditioning, telephone, cable TV, continental breakfast, restaurant-bar, exercise gym, and whirlpool tub.

Take a break from the sun beneath the shady streetfront awning of the **Restaurant El Tejado** (8 A.M.–8 P.M. daily, $4–8), on the main street next to Banamex. (You may need to ask the staff to kindly turn the TV off or at least lower the volume.)

For more economical but wholesome country cooking, check out the *fondas* (foodstalls) on side street Constitución de 1814, adjacent to the Ruta Paraíso bus station lot, and on side street Corregidora, the next block north.

Travel Agent

A competent and conveniently situated travel agency (and potential information source) is **Viajes Reyna Pío** (Av. L. Cárdenas, tel. 753/532-3868 or 753/532-3935, fax 753/532-0723), right across from the Ruta Paraíso bus station and Banamex.

Money Exchange

Change your money at one of three banks, all with ATMs, clustered nearby. **Banamex** (Av. L. Cárdenas 1646, tel. 753/532-2020, 9 A.M.–4 P.M. Mon.–Fri., 10 A.M.–2 P.M. Sat.). If it's too crowded, try **Bancomer** (Av. L. Cárdenas 1555, tel. 753/532-3888, 9 A.M.–4 P.M. Mon.–Fri., 10 A.M.–2 P.M. Sat.), a block north and across the street; or **Banco Santander Serfín** (Av. L. Cárdenas 1681, tel. 753/532-0032, 9 A.M.–4 P.M. Mon.–Fri., 10 A.M.–2 P.M. Sat.), on the same side half a block farther north.

Communications

The *correo* (tel. 753/537-2387) is in the middle of the big grassy town plaza; look for it on the left as you arrive at the town center, two long blocks after the big traffic circle.

Telecomunicaciones, with telegraph, money orders, telephone, and public fax (753/532-0273), is next door to the post office. For telephone, plenty of public street phones accept widely available Ladatel telephone cards. More expensive, but with long hours, is the computer-assisted long-distance telephone and fax agency **Computel** (Av. L. Cárdenas 1810, tel./fax 753/532-4806, fax 753/532-4807, 7:30 A.M.–10 P.M. daily), next to the Ruta Paraíso bus station at the corner of Constitución de 1814.

Connect to the Internet at the small store **Internet Sin Limite** (tel. 753/532-1480, 9 A.M.–10 P.M. Mon.–Sat.), corner of Javier Mina, across the street and south of Bancomer.

Health
The **General Hospital** (tel. 753/532-0900, 753/532-0901, 753/532-0902, 753/532-0903, or 753/532-0904), known locally as "Seguro Social," is on the boulevard into town, left side, corner of H. Escuela Naval, a block before the big right-side traffic circle. Alternatively, visit highly recommended **Dr. Gustavo Cejos Pérez** (Melchor Ocampo 475, tel. 753/532-3902). For routine medicines and drugs, go to conveniently situated **Farmacia Pronto** (tel. 753/537-5002, 8 A.M.–10 P.M. daily), a few doors north of the Ruta Paraíso bus station.

Getting There and Away
By car or RV, the options to and from Lázaro Cárdenas are virtually the same as those for Ixtapa and Zihuatanejo. Simply add or subtract the 50 miles (80 km) or 1.25-hour travel difference between Ixtapa or Zihuatanejo and Lázaro Cárdenas.

By bus, a trio of long-distance bus terminals serves Lázaro Cárdenas travelers. From the Ruta Paraíso (officially, Lineas Unidas del Sur) terminal (Av. L. Cárdenas 1810, tel. 753/532-0262 or 753/537-3868), **Ruta Paraíso** first-class and second-class local-departure buses connect north daily with Apatzingán, Uruapan, Pátzcuaro, and Morelia. Very frequent local departures also connect northwest along the coast with nearby coastal destinations of La Mira, Playa Azul, and Caleta de Campos. Additionally, several more first- and second-class departures connect northwest with long-distance destinations of Manzanillo and intermediate points. In an adjacent booth inside the station, agents (tel. 753/532-3006) sell tickets for **Parhikuni** luxury-class buses (with a/c waiting lounge), connecting north with Michoacán destinations of Nueva Italia, Uruapan, Pátzcuaro, and Morelia.

Directly across the street, **La Linea** (tel. 753/537-1850) and associated lines maintains a small streetfront station. It offers four types of departures: executive class "Plus," connecting northeast with Guadalajara via Tecomán and Colima; first- and second-class **Sur** buses, connecting north with Uruapan and Zamora and continuing west to Guadalajara; first-class Autovia 2000 buses, connecting north, via Uruapan and Morelia, thence east with Toluca and Mexico City; and second-class Autobuses Sur de Jalisco connecting northwest with Manzanillo and also with Guadalajara, via Colima and Ciudad Guzmán.

The big **Estrella Blanca** terminal (tel. 753/532-1171) is two short blocks away, directly behind the Ruta Paraíso terminal, on Francisco Villa between Constitución de 1814 and Corregidora. From there, one or two daily first-class local departures connect north with Michoacán destinations of Uruapan, Morelia, and Mexico City. Three first-class buses stop, en route southeast to Zihuatanejo, Acapulco, and the Oaxaca coast, and northwest to Manzanillo, Puerto Vallarta, Mazatlán, and the U.S. border. In addition, three Futura luxury-class local departures connect daily with Mexico City.

MOON IXTAPA & ZIHUATANEJO

Avalon Travel
a member of the Perseus Books Group
1700 Fourth Street
Berkeley, CA 94710, USA
www.moon.com

Editors: Kevin McLain, Annie M. Blakley
Series Manager: Kathryn Ettinger
Copy Editor: Amy Scott
Graphics Coordinator: Elizabeth Jang
Production Coordinator: Elizabeth Jang
Cover Designer: Elizabeth Jang
Map Editor: Kevin Anglin
Cartographers: Chris Markiewicz, Jon Niemczyk,
   Kat Bennett

ISBN-13: 978-1-59880-533-8

Some photos and illustrations are used by permission and are the property of the original copyright owners.

Front cover photo: View of church from rocky stairwell, Xcaret © istockphoto.com
Title page photo: Playa La Ropa, Zihuatanejo © istockphoto.com

Printed in United States

ABOUT THE AUTHOR

Bruce Whipperman

In the early 1980s, the lure of travel drew Bruce Whipperman away from a 20-year career of teaching physics. The occasion was a trip to Kenya, which included a total solar eclipse and a safari. He hasn't stopped traveling since.

With his family grown, he has been free to let the world's wild, beautiful corners draw him onward: the ice-clawed Karakoram, the Gobi Desert's trellised oases, Rajasthan's pink palaces, Japan's green wine country, Bali's emerald terraces, and Oaxaca's vibrant marketplaces.

Bruce has always pursued his travel career for the fun of it. He started with slide shows and photo gifts for friends. Others wanted his photos, so he began selling them. Once, stranded in Ethiopia, he began to write. A dozen years later, after scores of magazine and newspaper feature stories, *Moon Pacific Mexico* became his first book, and Moon Handbooks to Oaxaca, Puerto Vallarta, Guadalajara, and Acapulco, Ixtapa & Zihuatanejo followed.

For Bruce, travel writing heightens his awareness of the places he visits and helps him focus his own travel experiences. He'll always remember what a Nepali Sherpa once said: "Many people come, looking, looking; few people come, see."

Travel, after all, is for returning home, and each adventure brings a tired but happy Bruce back to his friends, family, and loving wife, Gundi, in Berkeley, California.